Learning ArcGIS Geodatabases

An all-in-one start up kit to author, manage,
and administer ArcGIS geodatabases

Hussein Nasser

PUBLISHING

BIRMINGHAM - MUMBAI

Learning ArcGIS Geodatabases

First published: June 2014

Production reference: 1180614

Published by Packt Publishing Ltd.
Livery Place
35 Livery Street
Birmingham B3 2PB, UK.

ISBN 978-1-78398-864-8

www.packtpub.com

Cover image by Pratyush Mohanta (tysoncinematics@gmail.com)

Credits

Author
Hussein Nasser

Reviewers
Hani M. Basheer
Frank Donnelly
Venkatesh Merwade

Commissioning Editor
Kunal Parikh

Acquisition Editor
Subho Gupta

Content Development Editor
Akshay Nair

Technical Editor
Ankita Thakur

Copy Editors
Mradula Hegde
Dipti Kapadia
Stuti Srivastava

Project Coordinator
Sageer Parkar

Proofreader
Paul Hindle

Indexer
Rekha Nair

Graphics
Yuvraj Mannari

Production Coordinator
Shantanu Zagade

Cover Work
Shantanu Zagade

About the Author

Hussein Nasser is an Esri award-winning senior GIS solution architect at Electricity and Water Authority, Bahrain. He was the first author to write about the ArcGIS for Server technology after its complete revamp in Version 10.1. In 2007, Hussein won the annual ArcGIS for Server Code Challenge conducted at the Esri Developer Summit in Palm Springs, California, for using the AJAX technology with ArcGIS for Server, which was not implemented back then. His eight-year career as a GIS architect at the leading Middle Eastern engineering company Khatib & Alami involved implementing various utility GIS systems based on the Esri technology across the Middle East. After this, Hussein decided to move to a more focused environment at Electricity and Water Authority, Bahrain, his homeland, where he could channel his expertise to develop a robust GIS utility solution and fully integrate it with the e-government project, which would help Bahrain march towards the smart grid. Beyond GIS, Hussein is fascinated by acute research topics. Among the papers he is currently working on are *The Human API: A Software Interface to Prevent Cancer*, *Global Economic Crisis and Natural Disasters Quantum Detector*, and the *Stock Market and the Moon Phases*.

To Nada: "May all our dreams come true."

About the Reviewers

Hani M. Basheer is a GIS expert and Oracle certified professional DBA. He graduated in the year 2001 as a surveying engineer with a technical postgraduate diploma in Esri GIS. He has over 15 years of experience in the field of Geographic Information Systems (GIS), Esri products.

Throughout his career, he has worked on several enterprise GIS projects in Egypt and Saudi Arabia; he worked with the Egypt SDI project, which is a project to establish a GIS system for the NARSS and EMRA authorities in Egypt. He moved to Saudi Arabia in 2007 to work with a leading GIS company, FarsiGeoTech, which deals with many GIS projects. Hani moved to National Water Company in 2010 to establish a GIS unit, GIS model, geodatabase, and GIS application to manage the water and waste water utility networks of Jeddah city.

Hani has over 10 years of experience as a technical trainer for GIS products. During this period, he has delivered many successful training sessions in the Middle East to different sectors such as petroleum, mining, education, electricity, and municipalities.

Throughout his career, he has worked with most Esri products. He worked with Oracle databases and earned four DBA OCPs. He has also worked with SAN storage, GPS, and GPS CORS systems.

He really liked this book. While reviewing, he found it interesting enough to complete it from start to end. He also felt that the writer succeeded in providing knowledge to the readers in an easy way. He guarantees the readers that they will get the best out of their GIS career by reading this book.

I would like to thank my wife, Wegdan, for her love and support. I also want to acknowledge my loving family, who are always there for me.

Frank Donnelly is a Geospatial Data Librarian at Baruch College, City University of New York, where he assists students and faculty with finding and processing data and using GIS. He holds master's degrees in both Geography and Library and Information Science. He has been using GIS for over 15 years and has extensive experience working with the US Census data. He has built several spatial databases using ArcGIS personal geodatabases and open source SpatiaLite, including a geodatabase for studying New York City neighborhoods, which is freely available on his college's website. He has recently published papers on the geography of public libraries in the United States and the use of the US Census Bureau's American Community Survey for research.

Venkatesh Merwade is an associate professor at the Lyles School of Civil Engineering, Purdue University. His research and teaching interests include solving water resources issues by using GIS, computer modeling, and hydrologic information systems. His online tutorials, which are available at his website for free, on GIS applications and hydraulic and hydrologic modeling are used by students, researchers, and practitioners around the world to address water resource issues. He has co-authored two chapters in *Arc Hydro: GIS for Water Resources, Esri Press*; one chapter in *GIS, Spatial Analysis, and Modeling, Esri Press*; and one chapter in *Gravel Bed Rivers 7: Developments in Earth Surface Processes, Wiley*.

www.PacktPub.com

Support files, eBooks, discount offers, and more

You might want to visit www.PacktPub.com for support files and downloads related to your book.

Did you know that Packt offers eBook versions of every book published, with PDF and ePub files available? You can upgrade to the eBook version at www.PacktPub.com and as a print book customer, you are entitled to a discount on the eBook copy. Get in touch with us at service@packtpub.com for more details.

At www.PacktPub.com, you can also read a collection of free technical articles, sign up for a range of free newsletters and receive exclusive discounts and offers on Packt books and eBooks.

http://PacktLib.PacktPub.com

Do you need instant solutions to your IT questions? PacktLib is Packt's online digital book library. Here, you can access, read and search across Packt's entire library of books.

Why subscribe?

- Fully searchable across every book published by Packt
- Copy and paste, print and bookmark content
- On demand and accessible via web browser

Free access for Packt account holders

If you have an account with Packt at www.PacktPub.com, you can use this to access PacktLib today and view nine entirely free books. Simply use your login credentials for immediate access.

Table of Contents

Preface

When the publisher asked me to write a book about ArcGIS geodatabases, I was glad to do so. I have been working with geodatabases since 2005 with eight different versions of ArcGIS starting from Version 9.1; writing this title was a thrill for me. When the publisher mentioned that they need it to be a short book, based on the research done by their strategy team, I had to put in an extra effort and make tough decisions on what to include in this book and what to discard, without compromising on the quality of the content. What you are holding in your hands now is the essence of that work.

Learning ArcGIS Geodatabases was designed for those who want to start using the ArcGIS technology or those who have been using it and want to learn more about geodatabases. There are going to be three themes that will run throughout the book. The first theme covers *Chapter 1, Authoring Geodatabases*, and *Chapter 2, Working with Geodatabase Datasets*, and it is tailored for beginners and readers who are not familiar with ArcGIS geodatabases. It teaches readers how to author geodatabases and how to create and work with different datasets in their geodatabase. The second theme covers *Chapter 3, Modeling Geodatabases*, and *Chapter 4, Optimizing Geodatabases*, and it is targeted for intermediate users. It caters to those who know about geodatabases already and want to run them better. It is an excellent chapter for those who want to remodel their existing geodatabase and make it more efficient and cost less to maintain. They are also presented with new tools to help them tune and optimize their geodatabase. The last theme covers the last two chapters, *Chapters 5, Programming Geodatabases*, and *Chapter 6, Enterprise Geodatabases*, and it is designed for advanced readers. It caters to those who want to excel in using ArcGIS geodatabases with programming and script writing to manage and administer their geodatabase. They want to upgrade and use enterprise geodatabases instead of using simple file geodatabases so they can get the benefits of the multiuser environment.

All three themes come under the umbrella of a project called Bestaurants, where the reader helps a client in Belize, a country on the northeastern coast of Central America. The reader will help improve the Bestaurants project by designing a geodatabase to visualize the best restaurants, diners, cafes, and so on in Belize. With each chapter, the Bestaurants client will ask for new requirements that the reader will try to implement by the end of the chapter. The reader will author the geodatabase, tune, optimize, and create additional datasets, and so much more as the requirements of the client increase.

What this book covers

Chapter 1, Authoring Geodatabases, introduces the concept of geodatabases and how you can design and create one using ArcGIS for Desktop. The chapter discusses a project, Bestaurants, where you need to create a file geodatabase for the restaurants in Belize to help the client visualize them on a map.

Chapter 2, Working with Geodatabase Datasets, will bring in new requirements for the Bestaurants project where you will learn how to create feature classes, tables, and relations between datasets in the geodatabase you created in *Chapter 1, Authoring Geodatabases.*

Chapter 3, Modeling Geodatabases, will show you some flaws of the design used while creating the geodatabase in *Chapter 1, Authoring Geodatabases.* It will teach you how to remodel your Bestaurants geodatabase in a more elegant way. It will also show you how to cut down the number of datasets to reduce future maintenance on the geodatabase.

Chapter 4, Optimizing Geodatabases, is where you will be given some new tools to optimize your Bestaurants geodatabase now that it has been modeled elegantly. You will learn concepts such as indexing, compacting, and compressing, which will help you optimize your geodatabase queries and maintain a healthy geodatabase.

Chapter 5, Programming Geodatabases, will take you further along your Bestaurants geodatabase by writing Python scripts against it. It will also teach you how to use a model builder to combine different geodatabase tools to save a lot of time in administering and maintaining your geodatabase.

Chapter 6, Enterprise Geodatabases, introduces the concept of enterprise geodatabases, an upgraded version of a geodatabase that supports multiple user access, enhanced security, and higher availability. It will show you how to set up and configure your enterprise geodatabase from scratch using Microsoft SQL Server Express and migrate your existing Bestaurants geodatabase to the new geodatabase.

What you need for this book

You need Esri ArcGIS for Desktop 10.2.x or 10.1. The book uses ArcGIS 10.2. You can download a trial at `http://www.esri.com/software/arcgis/trial` or order from your local Esri distributor.

Gliffy is an online modeling tool that can be accessed at `http://www.gliffy.com/`.

Microsoft SQL Server Express 2012 SP1 can be downloaded for free at `http://qr.net/mssqlexpress`.

Microsoft .Net Framework 3.5 SP1 can be downloaded for free at `http://qr.net/dnfm35sp1`.

Who this book is for

Whether you are a student, GIS user, analyst, DBA, system administrator, or programmer with basic or no knowledge of Esri GIS, this book is for you. The book is tailored for students who want to learn about ArcGIS geodatabase. However, down the road in the later chapters, the book helps readers who are looking to improve their existing geodatabases or those who want to use scripting, model builders, or even migrate to enterprise geodatabases.

Conventions

In this book, you will find a number of styles of text that distinguish between different kinds of information. Here are some examples of these styles, and an explanation of their meaning.

Code words in text, database table names, folder names, filenames, file extensions, pathnames, dummy URLs, user input, and Twitter handles are shown as follows: "Using Windows Explorer, create a folder named `c:\gdb`."

A block of code is set as follows:

```
import arcpy
import os
import datetime
sgdb_path = "c:/gdb/web"
sgdb_name = "Web_Bestaurants.gdb"
arcpy.CreateFileGDB_management(sgdb_path, sgdb_name)
sfc_source = "c:/gdb/Bestaurants_new.gdb/Food_and_Drinks"
sfc_dest = sgdb_path + "/" + sgdb_name + "/Restaurants"
```

```
#Copy features
arcpy.CopyFeatures_management (sfc_source, sfc_dest)
sfield_rating = "RATING"
sfield_desc = "DESCRIPTION"
arcpy.DeleteField_management(sfc_dest, sfield_rating)
arcpy.DeleteField_management(sfc_dest, sfield_desc)
input ("Web Bestaurants geodatabase created successfully, press any
key to continue.")
```

When we wish to draw your attention to a particular part of a code block, the relevant lines or items are set in bold:

```
import arcpy
import os
import datetime
sgdb_path = "c:/gdb/web"
sgdb_name = "Web_Bestaurants.gdb"
todaydate = str(datetime.date.today().year) + str(datetime.date.
today().month)  + str(datetime.date.today().day)
os.rename (sgdb_path + "/" + sgdb_name , sgdb_path + "/" + "Web_
Bestaurants" + todaydate + ".gdb")
```

New terms and **important words** are shown in bold. Words that you see on the screen, in menus or dialog boxes for example, appear in the text like this: "In the **Type** drop-down list, select **Point Features** to create the feature class with point geometry."

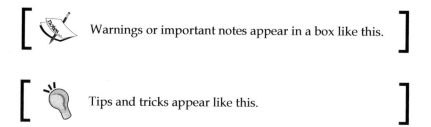

> Warnings or important notes appear in a box like this.

> Tips and tricks appear like this.

Reader feedback

Feedback from our readers is always welcome. Let us know what you think about this book—what you liked or may have disliked. Reader feedback is important for us to develop titles that you really get the most out of.

To send us general feedback, simply send an e-mail to feedback@packtpub.com, and mention the book title via the subject of your message.

If there is a topic that you have expertise in and you are interested in either writing or contributing to a book, see our author guide on www.packtpub.com/authors.

Customer support

Now that you are the proud owner of a Packt book, we have a number of things to help you to get the most from your purchase.

Downloading the example code

You can download the example code files for all Packt books you have purchased from your account at http://www.packtpub.com. If you purchased this book elsewhere, you can visit http://www.packtpub.com/support and register to have the files e-mailed directly to you.

Errata

Although we have taken every care to ensure the accuracy of our content, mistakes do happen. If you find a mistake in one of our books—maybe a mistake in the text or the code—we would be grateful if you would report this to us. By doing so, you can save other readers from frustration and help us improve subsequent versions of this book. If you find any errata, please report them by visiting http://www.packtpub.com/submit-errata, selecting your book, clicking on the **errata submission form** link, and entering the details of your errata. Once your errata are verified, your submission will be accepted and the errata will be uploaded on our website, or added to any list of existing errata, under the Errata section of that title. Any existing errata can be viewed by selecting your title from http://www.packtpub.com/support.

Piracy

Piracy of copyright material on the Internet is an ongoing problem across all media. At Packt, we take the protection of our copyright and licenses very seriously. If you come across any illegal copies of our works, in any form, on the Internet, please provide us with the location address or website name immediately so that we can pursue a remedy.

Please contact us at copyright@packtpub.com with a link to the suspected pirated material.

We appreciate your help in protecting our authors, and our ability to bring you valuable content.

Questions

You can contact us at questions@packtpub.com if you are having a problem with any aspect of the book, and we will do our best to address it.

1
Authoring Geodatabases

For a very long time, mankind recorded historical events in the form of drawings, inscriptions, and books. Books were organized into physical volumes, and volumes were arranged by their topic on shelves in a library. This system worked very well for centuries. We can place as many books as the shelf space can handle. With the information age and the invention of the byte, data is stored and retrieved electronically. It started with simple sequential text files. As more complex structures were introduced, we started depending on computers to store our data. This required a completely new system to structure, organize, and manage the digital data. For this, a system by which computers can efficiently browse and retrieve stored information was required, which led to the invention of the database.

A database is an organized collection of related data that's designed for efficient storage and retrieval. In this system, data is stored in a series of relations called tables. Each table contains a set of related data, where a row contains one instance of data and a column contains information that describes that instance.

Many **database management systems (DBMS)** have been introduced over the years. They have all been designed to organize digital information. When networking came into the picture, DBMSs evolved; now, multiple users can read the same piece of information from different locations (or from different continents). They can update the same table; therefore, the multiediting environment, database replications, and other niche technologies spawned from this field.

DBMS is a software that allows multiple users to interact with a database. They come either in the client-server model or the file-based model. These may include the server, which manages the database and listens for incoming client connections, and the client, which connects to the server.

After that short tour of the evolution of databases, we need to focus on the topic of this book. A database is a fascinating storage system. It allows you to retrieve, store, and edit different types of information such as text, images, music, and videos. However, for people like us who work with maps, we feel there is a missing element in that compound, that is, location. Adding location information to a database helps applications bring life to the tabular records in the database and make it available visually. For instance, you can add x and y columns to a Restaurant table in a database, which represents the coordinate's location of each restaurant in the table. Then, you can write a custom application to read the coordinates and display the restaurants in a map. Esri realized the importance of injecting location information into a database, and created its own standard location-based database; you guessed it, the ArcGIS geodatabase. An ArcGIS geodatabase offers you a generous number of geographically enabled objects called datasets.

An ArcGIS geodatabase is the proprietary database for Esri. All Esri geospatial software is built around this geodatabase.

In this chapter, you will work on a real-life business case study where you will learn how to create your first ArcGIS geodatabase and add different datasets using ArcGIS for Desktop, hereafter known simply as Desktop (uppercase). To start with this chapter, make sure you have a machine with Desktop 10 or higher. You can work with a 9.2.x or 9.3.x Version of Desktop since the underlying geodatabase is the same; however, you might be missing some features that are required to perform the exercises of the book. I will be using Version 10.2; you can download the latest version of ArcGIS for Desktop for free with a 60 day trial from the Esri website at http://www.esri.com/software/arcgis/arcgis-for-desktop/free-trial. You will need at least a standard or an advanced license, which will allow you to edit.

The ArcGIS geodatabases authored in 9.2 and 9.3.x can be viewed and edited in ArcGIS 10.x. However, it is recommended that you use 10.x geodatabases during the course of this book to maintain a consistent flow and error free exercises.

Bestaurants, the best restaurants in Belize

Belize thrives on tourism. Lots of tourists go there on holiday to enjoy its beautiful beaches and a wide range of restaurants. The government of Belize is trying to enrich tourists' experience by helping them to find their favorite restaurants in the country more effectively. To accomplish that, a new project titled **Bestaurants** has been proposed to design a new geodatabase which will have all places to eat and drink in Belize. Using ArcGIS for Desktop, we will design and create an ArcGIS geodatabase that can accommodate all diners, cafes, restaurants, bars, and lounges in Belize. You should be able to use Desktop to populate the geodatabase and add new venues in the Bestaurants geodatabase.

 This project is an example that will be used and will reappear in later chapters. It is not an actual project and is not related to the country whatsoever.

Designing the geodatabase schema

Before we start creating the geodatabase, we need to design a template that includes the tables, fields, and data types for the Bestaurants project. This template is called the geodatabase schema.

 A schema is a metadata template that describes the tables, fields, and field types in a particular database.

So, let's design the logical schema for the Bestaurants project. We will start with a very simple design where we create the basic atom dataset in the geodatabase, the feature class.

 The feature class is one of the basic objects in a geodatabase. This object class is a table with a shape attribute, which could be a point, line, or a polygon.

According to the case study, we need to create a geodatabase that accommodates diners, cafes, restaurants, bars, and lounges. So, we can create each one of them in a separate feature class, and then we need to give appropriate fields for each feature class. Take a few moments to answer these questions: what feature classes will you include in the geodatabase? What attributes will you use for each class? What are the data types for these attributes? Take a look at the following table:

Feature class	Field	Field type
Diners	NAME	Text
	WEBSITE	Text
	RATING	Short Integer
	SHAPE	Geometry
Cafes	NAME	Text
	WEBSITE	Text
	RATING	Short Integer
	SHAPE	Geometry
Restaurants	NAME	Text
	WEBSITE	Text
	CUISINE	Text
	RATING	Short Integer
	SHAPE	Geometry
Bars_and_Lounges	NAME	Text
	WEBSITE	Text
	RATING	Short Integer
	SHAPE	Geometry

There are a lot of ways to design the schema for a geodatabase. There are really good ways that keep your geodatabase healthy in the long run, and there are bad ways that are inefficient. This design is a simple one; it is not the ultimate, and you might come up with a better design. The only reason I selected this is for its simplicity, and there is definitely plenty of room for improvement. You will learn how to create an efficient schema design in *Chapter 3, Modeling Geodatabases,* as you are introduced to more geodatabase datasets.

As you can see, we have merged the bars and lounges into one single feature class. We have used point geometry to represent these feature classes since it is easier to sketch, which could be identified with a **Global Positioning System (GPS)** device. These feature classes are also fast to draw, and we don't really care about the boundaries. However, it all depends on your requirements; whether it is necessary to identify the boundary of a certain feature or not. You may use polygon geometry if you want to.

GPS is a space-based satellite navigation system that provides location and time information, whereas a feature is a single record or object in a feature class which has a set of attributes and geometric shapes.

Creating the geodatabase

After we have designed the geodatabase schema, it is now time to author the geodatabase. In this section, we will use ArcCatalog to create the geodatabase. ArcCatalog is an application that allows us to author geodatabases, browse through them, add/delete datasets from geodatabases, and so on. To create your first geodatabase, perform the following steps:

1. Open **ArcCatalog**; you can find it in the **Start** menu under the **ArcGIS** folder, as explained in this chapter. The following screenshot illustrates this:

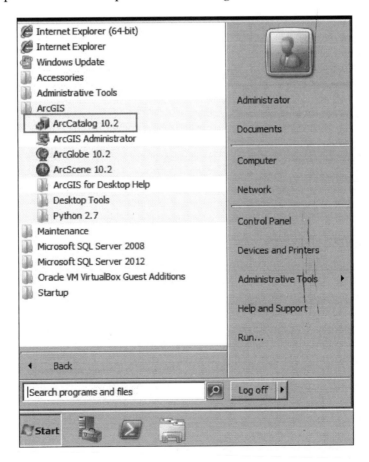

2. Once you start the application, make sure you see the **Catalog Tree** window. This is the folder view of your computer, and this is where we will be doing most of the work.

3. To show the **Catalog Tree** window, point the cursor to the **Windows** menu and then click on **Catalog Tree**.

4. Next, you need to specify the folder where you will create your `Restaurants` geodatabase.

5. Using Windows Explorer, create a folder named `c:\gdb`. This is where the geodatabase will go.

6. From the **Catalog Tree** window, right-click on the **Folder Connections** node and click on **Connect to Folder…**. This feature allows you to connect to your Windows folder.

7. Browse to the new folder you just created, `c:\gdb`, and then click on **OK**.

8. Select the folder and then right-click on the empty view to the right, point the cursor to **New**, then click on **File Geodatabase**, as shown in the following screenshot:

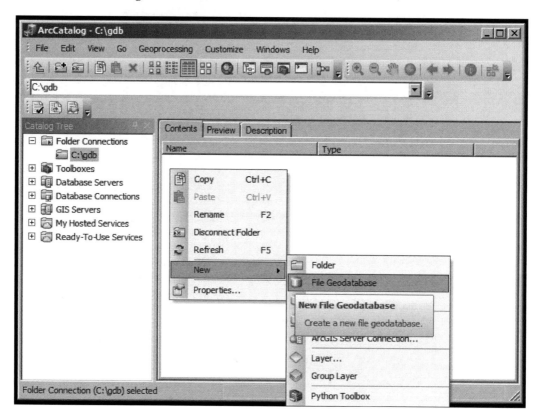

This will create a file geodatabase in the specified folder with a default name of New File Geodatabase.gdb; rename the new geodatabase to Bestaurants. The gdb extension is automatically appended.

 A file geodatabase is the proprietary geodatabase for Esri, structured as a folder with many files that can only be viewed and opened by Esri products or applications which support the file geodatabase API. This has an extension of gdb.

The spatial reference

Adding location information to a database requires two parameters, the actual location coordinates and how these coordinates are supposed to be drawn, which is also known as the spatial reference. The spatial reference describes whether the location is projected on a two- or three-dimensional map, and whether it should be defined for every dataset in the geodatabase that has a spatial component. While working in ArcMap, all datasets should share the same spatial reference.

 A spatial reference is a collection of properties that describe the system to locate a particular object in a coordinate system. You can find more information about this topic at http://bit.ly/lag_ spatialreference.

There are a lot of spatial references tailored for different locations on the Earth. There are some standard references used universally, and among them is the WGS 84, which we will be continuously using in this book.

Creating the feature classes

In the previous section, we designed the logical schema for our geodatabase. We will now create the actual datasets, or the physical schema. First, we start by creating the feature classes as follows:

1. Open **ArcCatalog** and browse to your Bestaurants geodatabase in the **Catalog Tree** window.

2. Click on the `Bestaurants` file geodatabase, right-click on the empty right panel, point the cursor to **New**, and then click on **Feature Class...**, as shown in the following screenshot:

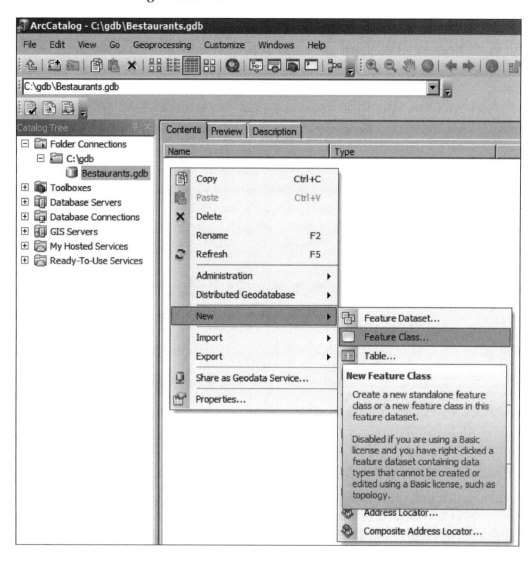

This will open up the **New Feature Class** dialog where you specify the basic properties of the feature class. In the **Name** field, type `Diners`. This is the physical name of the feature class in the geodatabase, and it should not contain special characters and should not include any spaces.

3. Type `Belize Diners` in the **Alias** field. This is a description of the feature class's name. It can be anything you want. When you add a new layer, it takes this alias name by default.

4. In the **Type** drop-down list, select **Point Features** to create the feature class with point geometry.

    The **Geometry Properties** section offers advanced options to enable the feature class. This includes the M value that helps in the route information for linear features and the Z value that is used for 3D representation, which enables the elevation and extrusion of features. The Z value can be useful, for example, if a restaurant is located on the 11th floor of the Ritz Carlton hotel.

> Besides X and Y coordinates, the M value can be added to each vertex on a line to provide more information, such as the direction.
>
> Unlike X and Y coordinates, the Z value can be considered as the height of a feature upward or downwards. This value can be assigned to features so they are represented in a 3D plane.

5. Since we don't need to store route or 3D data at this stage, leave the M and Z values unchecked. Click on **Next**. This is illustrated in the following screenshot:

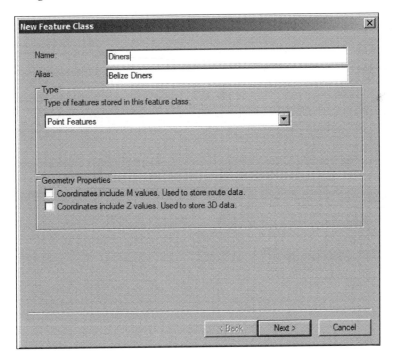

In the next dialog box, you will set the spatial reference for our new feature class. You will use the **WGS_1984_Web_Mercator** standard spatial reference, which is also used by Google Maps.

6. In the **spatial reference** drop-down list, select **WGS_1984_Web_Mercator** and press *Enter* to find its item.

7. Expand the **Projected Coordinate Systems** node, then expand the **World** node, and then click on the **WGS 1984 Web_Mercator (auxiliary sphere)** node, as illustrated in the following screenshot.

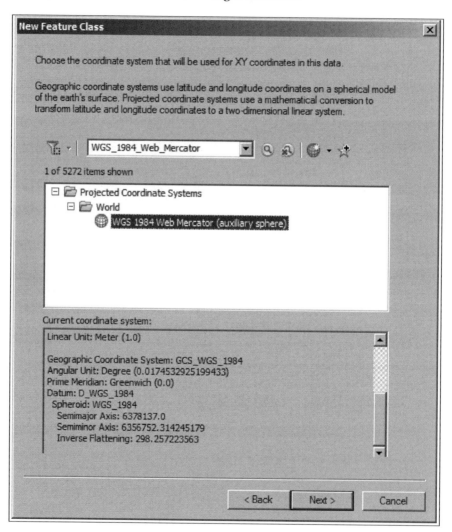

8. Click on **Next** to move to the next form.

   Next, we set the **XY Tolerance** value for the feature class. As you start adding features, you might want to add some features close to each other, but you don't want them to snap into the same position. In this case, make this value smaller to get a higher accuracy for each feature position. However, sometimes, you will need to add features on top of each other, making them overlap on purpose, especially if you have Z values. Too small a tolerance value might make it difficult to snap these features into a single location and might cause problems with shared boundaries.

9. As you can see, this value needs to be carefully planned, but for now, leave the **XY Tolerance** value to its default value, which is 0.001 meters, and click on **Next**.

> The **XY Tolerance** value is the minimum distance after which two features will snap together.

In the next form, we select the configuration keyword; choose the **Default** configuration keyword and click on **Next**.

> The configuration keyword is a table space in which feature classes and tables are stored. Each configuration has certain properties, such as the geometry type and file size, which are shared by all objects in that keyword.

Finally, we add the fields for our feature class. Note that two fields are already added for you. The first field is OBJECTID, which is also the primary key; a sequence number that represents each feature in the feature class uniquely.

> The primary key is a column by which a record is uniquely identified in a table or a dataset.

The second field is SHAPE, which if you remember, we have added by specifying the geometry type. So, we need to add three more fields: NAME, WEBSITE, and RATING; click on an empty row in the **Field Name** column and add the following fields:

Name	Data Type
NAME	Text
WEBSITE	Text
RATING	Short Integer

After adding all the fields, your dialog box should look like the following screenshot; click on **Finish** to create the feature class:

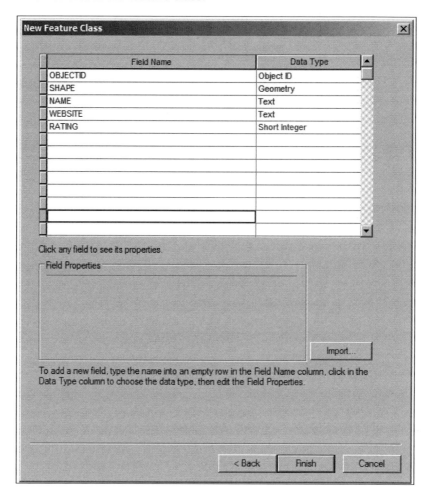

You just created your first feature class; if you take a look at the icon, you will see three small dots, which indicates that this feature class has a point geometry.

Using the same approach, create the rest of the feature classes, `Cafes`, `Restaurants`, and `Bars_and_Lounges`, in your geodatabase based on the schema we designed earlier.

> If you are creating multiple feature classes with similar fields, use the **Import...** feature in the fields' page to import the fields from an existing feature class. This could prove efficient when you are authoring your geodatabase.

After creating all the feature classes, your final geodatabase should look like the following screenshot:

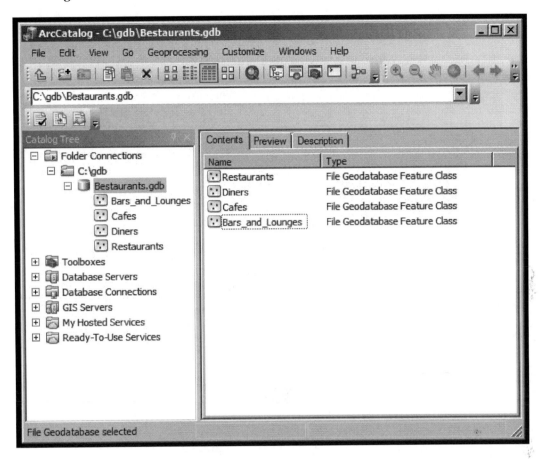

Editing the geodatabase in ArcMap

We have authored our Bestaurants geodatabase and created the food and drinks venues' feature classes. However, these classes are empty, and until they have some features, we can't visualize them; it is time to populate them with features. To do that, we need an editing tool, and ArcMap can help with this. However, before we can start editing our geodatabase, we need to know where we can add these features. We can't just place them anywhere in the world. We need a reference to base our editing on, Basemap. I have already prepared a map document and saved it to the extent of Belize. You can find it in the supporting files for this chapter, 86480T_01_Files, which can be downloaded from www.packtpub.com.

Basemap is a background map that usually references imagery and land information.

Browse to `86480T_01_Files\MapDocuments` and open the `Belize_BaseMap.mxd` file; this will open ArcMap. You will need an Internet connection for this exercise since the document connects to an online basemap. We will start by adding the `Restaurants` feature class. To do this, perform the following steps:

1. From the **ArcMap** menu, point the cursor to **File**, then **Add Data**, and click on **Add Data...**.

2. From the **Add Data** dialog box, expand the **Look in** drop-down list and select the `Bestaurants` geodatabase in `c:\gdb`.

3. Double-click on the `Restaurants` feature class to add it to ArcMap, as shown in the following screenshot:

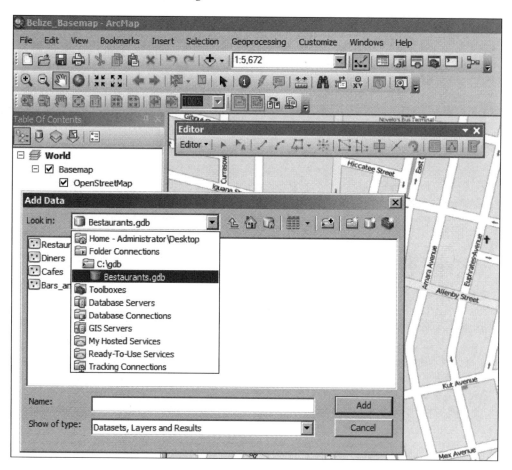

Notice that a new layer is added with the alias name of the feature class that we specified while creating it. Also, a default red point is added as a symbology for our feature class. Let's change it to a more relevant symbol by performing the following steps:

A layer is an ArcMap object and a visual representation of a physical feature class. A layer does not exist by itself and must have a source dataset to read data from.

A symbology is a notation for the features in a feature class. A given feature class might have multiple symbologies based on its attributes.

1. Double-click on the **Belize Restaurants** layer to view the **Layer Properties** dialog box.
2. Click on the **Symbology** tab.
3. In the **Symbol** section, click on the red dot and select a restaurant icon; type Restaurant in the filter box. The dialog box will look like the following screenshot:

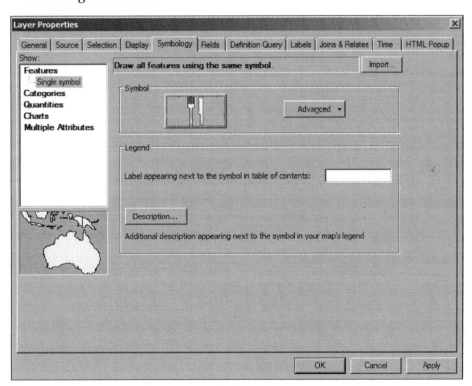

4. Close the **Layer Properties** dialog.

Now, it is time to add some features. Before we do so, make sure that you close ArcCatalog and that you do not have any connections to your geodatabase. Now, to display the **Editor** toolbar, perform the following steps:

1. Right-click on an empty area in the menu and select the **Editor** toolbar to activate it.

> The **Editor** toolbar will be displayed only if you have standard and advanced licenses. For details, refer to
> `http://www.esri.com/software/arcgis/about/`
> `gis-for-me`.

2. On the **Editor** toolbar, point the cursor to **Editor** and click on **Start Editing**.

3. Click on the **Create Features** button in the **Editor** toolbar, and you will see the **Create Feature** window pop up on the right-hand side.

4. Click on **Belize Restaurant** and add some restaurants on the Belize map; you don't have to be accurate at this stage. You should get something like what is shown in the following screenshot:

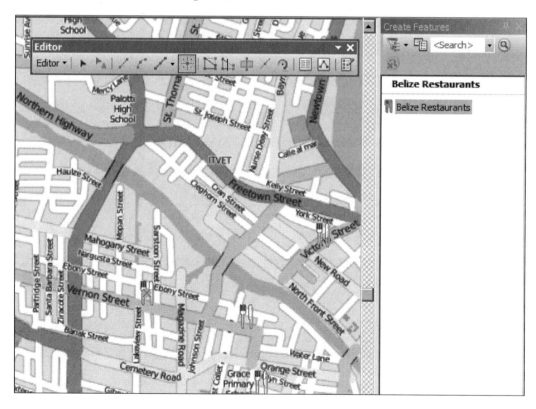

You can set the attributes for each feature you add by selecting that feature and clicking on the **Attribute** tool in the **Editor** toolbar. You can populate the rest of your geodatabase feature classes by adding the feature classes to the same map.

5. From the **Editor** toolbar, point the cursor to **Editor** and click on **Save Edits** if you wish to save your edits.

6. Close ArcMap.

Summary

In this chapter, you learned how to design, author, test, and edit a complete geodatabase by following a real-life example. You started with designing the schema of the geodatabase. You also specified the fields, data types, and geometry type for the feature classes. You then created the physical file geodatabase using ArcCatalog, specified the spatial reference, and used the editing tools in ArcMap to populate the geodatabase with features.

In the next chapter, you will enhance the skills acquired in this chapter to do more work with geodatabase datasets.

2
Working with Geodatabase Datasets

In the previous chapter, we discussed how to design and author an ArcGIS geodatabase. After reading and analyzing the Bestaurants case study, we created the geodatabase and populated it with feature classes based on the requirements. We even defined a spatial reference for the geodatabase so that our data is correctly projected. We then used ArcMap to edit the geodatabase and add some features to the feature class. In this chapter, we will delve deeper into the different types of geodatabase datasets, and work closely with each one and use them to enrich our Bestaurants geodatabase. Now that you know the basic tools to author geodatabases, let's equip you with a few more tools to do even more.

Working with feature classes

Let's start with the feature classes. We have already learned how to create a new feature class. In this section, we will learn how to add and delete attributes and work with the concept of subtypes and domains.

A subtype is a subset of the features in a given feature class sharing the same attributes.

A domain is a range of the possible values for a given attribute. It is usually used to avoid erroneous entries.

Adding new attributes

Your client for the Bestaurants project reviewed your initial geodatabase and suggested some changes. They noticed that you have a name field for each feature class, but they need to have the DESCRIPTION and REVIEW attributes, which can help the customers by giving them more descriptive information about a particular restaurant. To add these attributes, perform the following steps (make sure all instances of ArcMap and ArcCatalog are closed):

1. Open a fresh session of **ArcCatalog** and browse to the Bestaurants geodatabase. Start adding the two attributes to the **Diners** feature class.
2. Right-click on the **Diners** feature class and select **Properties**.
3. In the **Properties ...** dialog, select the **Fields** tab in case it is not already activated.
4. Click on the first empty row below the last field in the **Field Name** column and type DESCRIPTION. Select **Text** from the **Data Type** column.
5. Similarly, add the REVIEW attribute of the type **Text**.
6. Add the two fields to all the feature classes.
7. To delete an attribute, select it and hit the *Delete* key.

 You cannot add or delete a new attribute when the geodatabase is locked or is currently in use by ArcMap, for instance.

Leave **ArcCatalog** open as we will use it for the next topic where we will show you how to modify the properties of the attributes.

Modifying the properties of the attributes

Each attribute has its own properties, which we can change to fit our requirements; this is what we will be doing in this topic. We have both good and bad news. The good news is that the client was happy to see the new attributes during the testing session in ArcMap; however, when they tried to type in a review, they couldn't write more than 50 characters, which was a bit embarrassing. Also, they want to rename the attribute to be more descriptive, for instance, REVIEW should be Restaurant's Review or Diner's Review. We need to fix this. These are things that did not discuss in *Chapter 1, Authoring Geodatabases*, which are called field properties or attribute properties.

 Field properties are the metadata of a given attribute in a feature class, such as alias name, field size, and default value.

The default length for a text field in a geodatabase file is 50 characters. To modify the field size for the REVIEW field, perform the following steps:

1. Make sure all instances of ArcMap and ArcCatalog are closed.

2. Open a fresh session of **ArcCatalog** and browse to your geodatabase.

3. Open the **Properties...** dialog for the Diner feature class.

4. From the **Fields** tab, click on the attribute you want to modify; in this case, it is the REVIEW attribute.

5. Under **Field Properties**, type Diner's Review in the **Alias** field, and set the **Length** field to 3000 characters instead of 50, as illustrated in the following screenshot; this field length should be enough for a review:

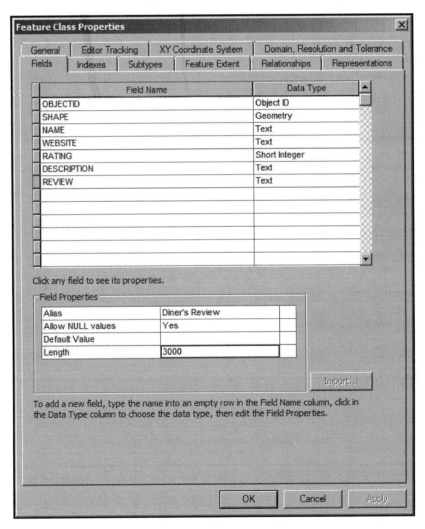

Let's go through the rest of the feature classes and update them with the latest changes. Also, make sure to update all the field alias names to initial case.

Domains

Excellent job with the new changes you introduced to the geodatabase! During the Bestaurant geodatabase's review workshop, the client pinpointed a small possible area for improvement when entering the rating for restaurants. They noticed that ArcMap allows any number for the rating without validating it. It would be better if the geodatabase can handle this kind of validation and allow the rating to be from 1 to 5 only.

To apply such kind of restrictions and ranges to an attribute, we will introduce a new useful tool to work with feature classes and domains. A domain is a property of the geodatabase shared by the individual datasets. This means it should be created on the geodatabase level and used on the datasets. There are two types of domains: coded values and ranged values. Coded values are discreet values, whereas ranged values allow a continuous range of values. Both the domain types have their applications; however, it seems that our case study can be solved with the coded domain.

We will now create a domain called RATING_SYSTEM, which will have the discreet values 1 to 5. To do this, perform the following steps:

1. Open **ArcCatalog** if it is not open and browse to the Bestaurants geodatabase.

2. Right-click on the Bestaurants geodatabase and select **Properties**. Make sure the **Domains** tab is activated.

3. Click on an empty record in the **Domain Name** column and type RATING_SYSTEM; optionally, you can type a description of this domain in the next column.

4. In the **Domain Properties** section, select **Short Integer** from the **Field Type** property, select **Coded Values** from the **Domain Type** property, and leave the rest as default values.

5. Fill the **Coded Values** section with the values given in the following table (code is what will be stored in the geodatabase physically, and description is what the editor will see in ArcMap when editing an attribute):

Code	Description
1	Poor
2	Fair
3	Average
4	Good
5	Excellent

Click on **Apply** and then click on **OK** to close the dialog.

This will create the domain in the geodatabase, which you can see in the next screenshot. However, we still have to do some work in the next sections as no feature class currently knows of this domain. Your end result should look like the following screenshot:

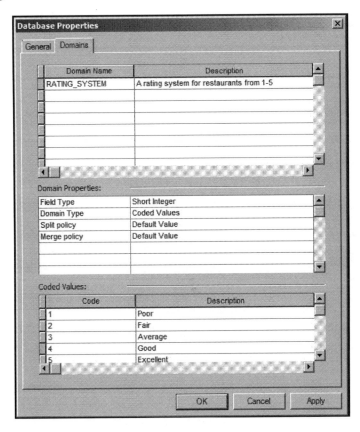

Next, we need to assign the domain we just created to the RATING field in each feature class. Right-click on the **Diners** feature class and select **Properties....** In the **Fields** tab, select the RATING field, and from **Field Properties** section, select RATING_SYSTEM in the **Domain** property.

 Note that the domain entry might not appear if the target field is not of the same data type as the domain.

Click on **Apply** and then click on **OK** to close the dialog and save the changes. The following screenshot explains the steps we just did:

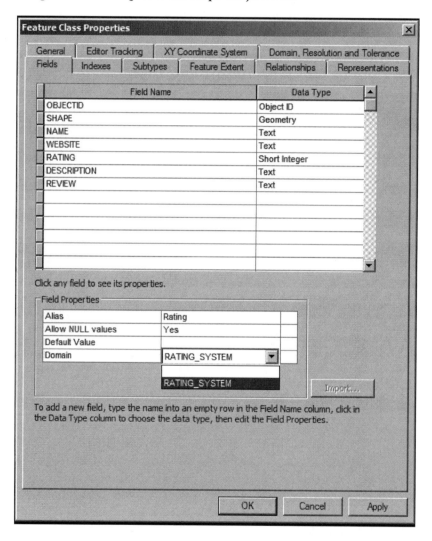

Let's test this. Open the `Belize_Basemap.mxd` file. You can find it in the supporting files for this chapter, `8648OT_02_Files`, which can be downloaded from `www.packtpub.com`. Perform the following set of steps in order to test the new domain we just added:

1. Add the `Diners` feature class and set the symbology like you did in *Chapter 1, Authoring Geodatabases*.

2. Open the **Editor** toolbar, point the cursor to **Editor**, and then click on **Start Editing**.

3. Add a new diner feature next to Vernon Street.

4. Click on the **Attributes** tab to set the attributes.

5. Set the **Diner's Name** field as `Ruby's Diner`.

6. For the **Rating** field, select **Good**; note that a drop-down list pops up for us to select from, as shown in the following screenshot:

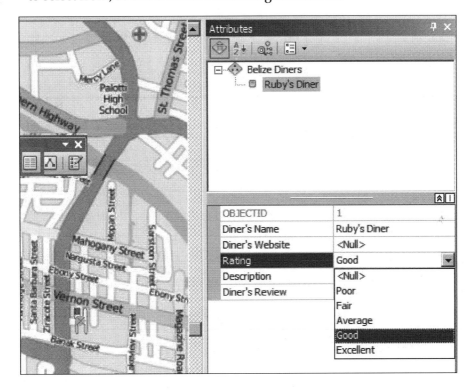

7. Save your edits and then save your `Belize_Basemap.mxd` file by clicking on the **File** menu and then on **Save**.

8. Close ArcMap.

Now, we can move to the next topic where we will add subtypes to our geodatabase.

Subtypes

Your geodatabase is getting better with each enhancement. We added new attributes to the feature classes and modified the properties of these attributes. We even assigned domains to the existing fields in order to reduce errors while creating features and to preserve data integrity. However, the client has one more request before we move on to the next phase. In the current geodatabase design, the bars and lounges were merged into one feature class; this made it difficult to differentiate bars from lounges. The solution to this might be obvious. We could add a new field named Category, then create a domain with two coded values, Bar and Lounge, assign this domain to the CATEGORY field, and we are done. This could definitely work; however, we will do it in a different way this time. We will break down the bars and lounges into different subtypes for the parent feature class, Bars_and_Lounges. Subtypes are helpful, especially while editing, since you can specify a default subtype with predefined default attributes.

Before we can create a subtype, we need a subtype field; so, we need to add this field. Unlike domains, a subtype field must be an integer. Perform the following steps to start adding your subtype:

1. Open **ArcCatalog** and browse to your geodatabase.

2. Right-click on the **Bars_and_Lounges** feature class and click on **Properties....** Then, select the **Fields** tab and add a new field of the **Short Integer** type and name it CATEGORY.

3. Click on **Apply** and then click on **OK**. Close the dialog so that the geodatabase gets updated with the new field. Don't close **ArcCatalog** yet; we still need to use it.

4. Now, we are ready to create our two subtypes. Open the **Bars_and_Lounges** properties and select the **Subtypes** tab.

5. From the **Subtype Field** drop-down list, select **CATEGORY** — the field we have just created.

6. You will notice that an entry is created with the code 0 and a new subtype. Let's rename the subtype to Bar and add a new entry with code 1 and name it Lounge.

7. You can click on each subtype and assign default values to them so that when a new feature of that particular subtype is created, the default values are automatically populated in the feature, saving a lot of time. See the following screenshot for more details:

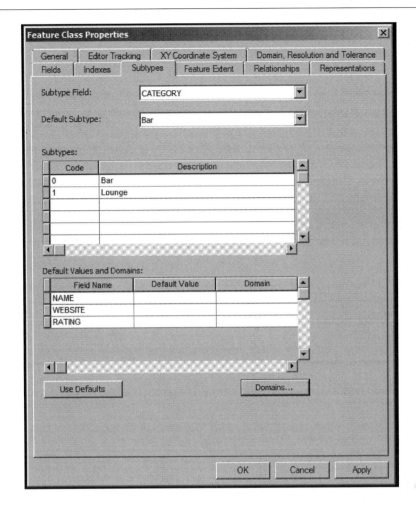

8. Click on **Apply** and then click on **OK** to close the dialog.

9. Close **ArcCatalog**.

Working with object tables and relations

A question was raised during the Bestaurants workshop review: what if I want to write multiple reviews for a given restaurant or diner? Does the geodatabase support that? The answer is no. We have a single review field for each feature. We can add another field called REVIEW2, for instance, but it is infeasible as we will end up with a very rigid geodatabase design. It is not an elegant solution to the multiple reviews problem. It seems that we can't work out a solution for this with the skills we have acquired so far while working with feature classes. We need a new tool that can help us tackle this. Here is where object tables come into the picture.

An object table is a table in the geodatabase that stores only the records without geometry.

Tables are extremely useful, and yes, we can create them in the geodatabase too! However, how can we use tables to solve the multiple reviews problem? For each restaurant, diner, and so on, there might be multiple reviews; so, one feature can have many reviews. Let's start with `Diners`; for this, we need to create the `DINERS_REVIEWS` table. To create the table, perform the following steps:

1. Open **ArcCatalog** and browse to your `Restaurants` geodatabase.

2. Right-click on the empty area on the right, point the cursor to **New**, and then select **Table**, as shown in the following screenshot:

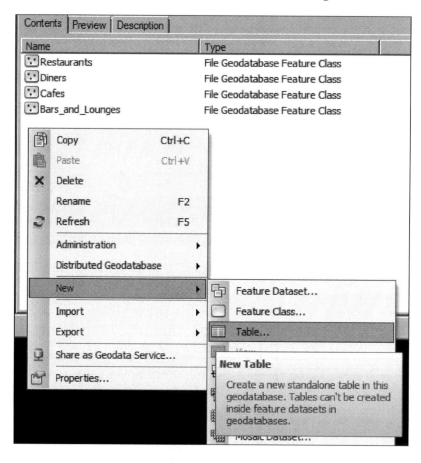

3. Type `DINER_REVIEWS` in the **Name** field and `Diners' Reviews` in the **Alias** field, as shown in the following screenshot, and then click on **Next**:

4. Use the default configurations and click on **Next**.

5. In the attributes dialog, add the two attributes, `REVIEW` of the type **Text** with a maximum length of 3000 characters, and the `REVIEW_DATE` attribute of type **Date**, which will store the date of when the review was added. The last attribute is `DINER_OBJECTID`, which points to the diner for which this review is created. This is illustrated in the following screenshot:

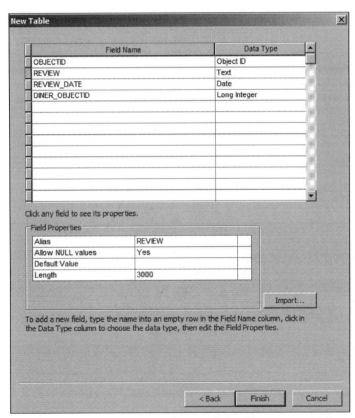

6. Click on **Finish** to create the table. Leave **ArcCatalog** open.

The REVIEWS table is created. This is where our multiple reviews will be stored. Still some element is missing; we didn't actually link this table to the Diners feature class. Naming the table Diner's Reviews isn't enough to link it to the Diners feature class. We should physically create what we call a relationship class.

 A relationship class is a class that links two datasets together in a geodatabase. It has an origin dataset and a destination dataset.

To create a relationship class, perform the following steps:

1. Select your geodatabase from **ArcCatalog** and right-click on an empty area; point the cursor to **New** and then select **Relationship Class...**, as shown in the following screenshot:

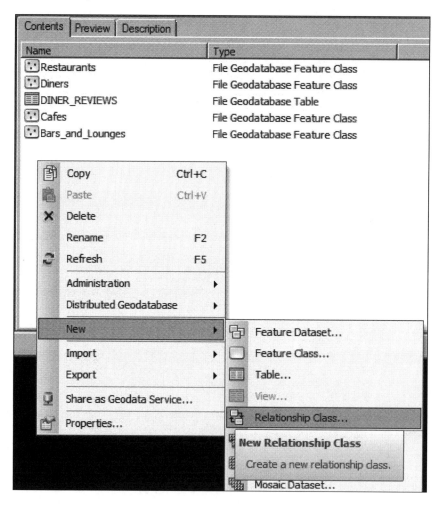

2. In the **New Relationship Class** dialog, type DINERS_REVIEWS_REL as the class name. The following screenshot illustrates how to perform this.

3. From the **Origin table/feature class** list, select the **Diners** feature class.

4. From the **Destination table/feature class** list, select the DINER_REVIEWS table, as shown in the following screenshot, and then click on **Next** to move to the next form:

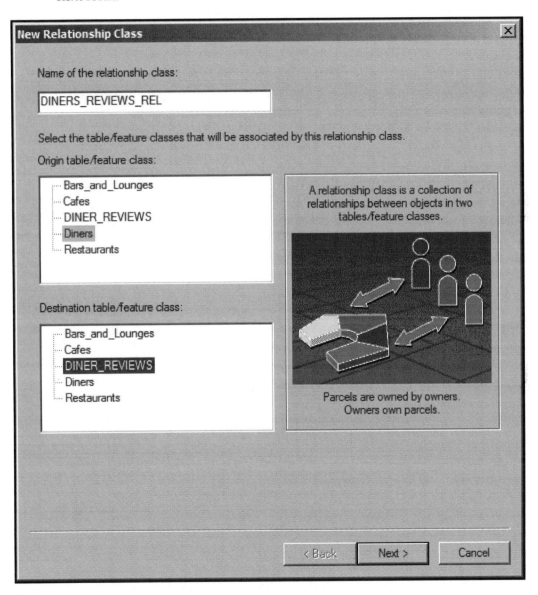

There are two types of bidirectional relationships between two objects: aggregation and composition. The simplest difference between them is that the aggregation relationship is independent. This means that deleting the origin object does not delete the related objects in the destination. It is also referred to as a simple peer-to-peer relation; for example, a vehicle and its engine. An engine can exist without a car, which means you can theoretically install that engine into another vehicle. A composition relationship is where a destination object cannot exist without an origin object. I don't really encounter many examples where a destination object cannot exist without an origin object; even when I do, I usually use an aggregation relation, just to keep my related records. You wouldn't want to delete related records in a production environment by deleting a single origin object. You would like to keep your destination objects so you can refer back to them anytime for the history.

For our reviews object, although this relationship does seem like a composition relation, we will use a simple peer-to-peer relation so that we can keep our reviews in case the diner is removed. In this dialog, select the **Simple (peer-to-peer) relationship** option and click on **Next**. In the next form, we will discuss the messages propagated between the origin and destination. Note that we have added the diner object ID on the reviews record, which is the many side of the relationship. Hence, the DINER_REVIEWS table will need to access the Diners feature class. We refer to this kind of messaging as backward messaging because the messages are propagated from the destination to the origin:

5. As illustrated in the following screenshot, select **Backward (destination to origin)** and click on **Next**:

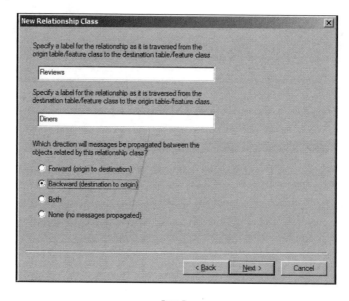

6. Select the **1-M (one to many)** relation and click on **Next**.

7. Next, you will be prompted whether you want to add new fields to the relations; select **No, I do not want to add attributes to this relationship class** and then click on **Next**.

8. This stage is very important. We will now select the fields that link the Diners feature class with the DINERS_REVIEWS table. The primary key of the origin (the DINERS feature class) is OBJECTID, and the related foreign key of the destination (the DINERS_REVIEWS table) is the one we created, which is DINERS_OBJECTID. Click on **Next**. All this is illustrated in the following screenshot:

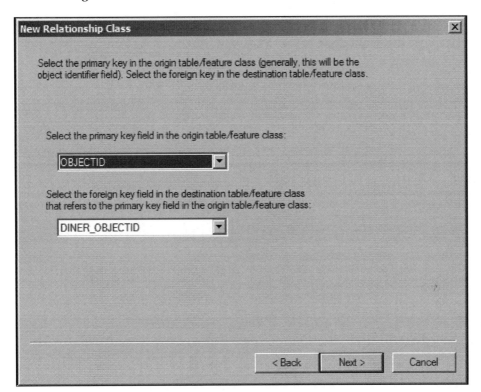

9. You will be presented with a summary. Click on **Finish** to create the relationship class. Your ArcCatalog should look like the one seen in the following screenshot after you finish:

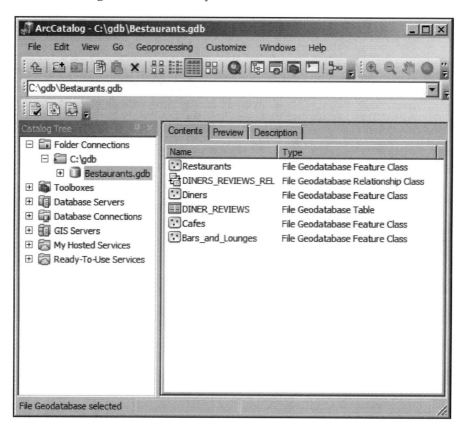

We just created a relationship between a feature class and an object table. We need ArcMap to test if the relation works:

1. Close **ArcCatalog** and open your modified `Belize_Basemap.mxd` file instead.

2. You should see your Diner's layer on the map as we have saved it before. In case you didn't save the document, you can add it again, similar to how we learned, by pointing to the **File** menu and then clicking on **Add Data...**. From the dialog, browse to your geodatabase, select **Diners**, and click on **Add**.

3. Bring up your **Editor** toolbar, point the cursor to **Editor**, and then click on **Start Editing** so that we can add a new diner.

4. From the right panel, activate the **Create Feature** tab and select **Belize Diners**.

5. Add a new diner next to **Ruby's Diner**. The new diner is named `Cran Street Diner`. Fill it with the attributes as shown in the following screenshot:

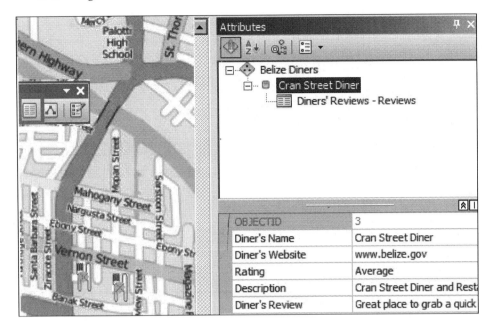

Take a look at the **Diner's Reviews – Reviews** relation that popped up while editing; this means that you can add a related review from here. To add a review, perform the following steps:

1. From the **Attributes** window, which is shown in the following screenshot, right-click on **Diner's Reviews – Reviews** and then click on **Add New**. This will add a new related record to the DINER_REVIEWS table.

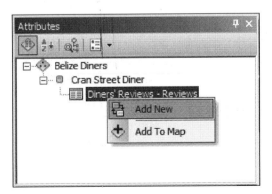

2. Click on the new object that is created and populate the record with the review as illustrated in the following screenshot (note how the diner object's ID is automatically assigned):

3. Point the cursor to **Editor** and then click on **Save Edits** to save your changes.

4. In ArcMap, point the cursor to **File** and then click on **Save** to save the `Belize_BaseMap.mxd` file.

You just finished creating the object tables with the relationship class.

To-do

Add three other reviews to this `Diner` feature class using the same approach. You can see your reviews when you identify the diner using the ArcMap identify tool.

Working with annotations

Once you complete the geodatabase, you may want to visualize it by creating a map. An important element of a map is labeling, where features are labeled based on their values, giving richness to the map. If you are familiar with ArcMap, you might have done labeling before. However, labeling is done in the map and labels are generated and placed dynamically. This might not be efficient for a large set of features. That's why we are interested in another method of labeling using what we call the annotation class.

> Labeling is a property of a map where a text label is placed on each feature, pointing to a single or a combination of attribute values in that feature.
>
> An annotation class is a geodatabase dataset used to label features in a feature class.

Our Belize client has asked us to label all their venues with their names. For this, we will use annotation. To do so, perform the following steps:

1. Open your `Belize_Basemap.mxd` file. You should see the Diner's layers as we saved it in the previous exercise.

2. Double-click on the **Belize Diners** layer to open the layer properties and select the **Labels** tab.

3. Check the **Label Features** option in this layer and then select **Diner's Name** from the **Label** drop-down list.

   Note how ArcMap displays a label on each feature; this could be enough and we can stop here. Labeling works on the client side. This puts more work on ArcMap, as software and the machine's ArcMap is installed only to render, color, and style the labels. With more features, map labeling is usually not the optimal way and can result in performance problems. That's why annotation is recommended. Annotations works on the server side, and they are brought to ArcMap ready to be displayed, which optimizes the map.

4. Creating an annotation is easy; simply right-click on the **Belize Diners** layer and click on **Convert Labels to Annotation...**, as you can see in the following screenshot:

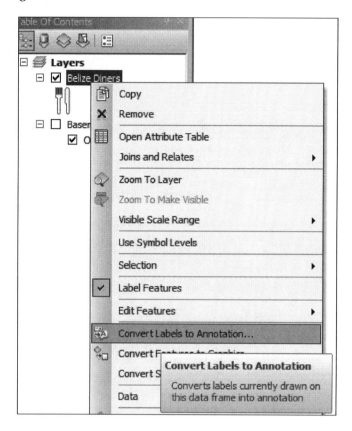

5. After this, a new dialog will pop up with details. You have the option to convert all the labels or just the ones in the current context. Leave the default options and click on **Convert** as illustrated in the following screenshot.

This will create the annotation class and the necessary relationship class to link them. This way, ArcMap does not have to do more work in labeling every single feature with its different font, color, and style, but instead simply queries the annotation class, retrieves them, and renders them on the map.

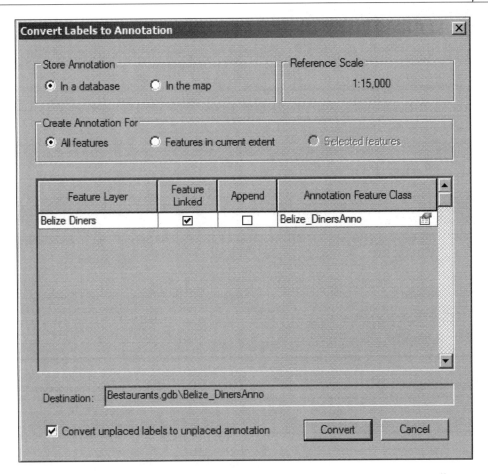

Importing other datasets

In real-life scenarios, you will not have to create all the data from scratch; some of the data will be available for you in different formats such as shape files, images, Excel sheets, and CAD files. That's why it is important to discuss how to import different kinds of formats to your geodatabase. In this section, we will discuss importing shape files, CAD files, and coverage classes that represent the boundary of Belize.

The client has asked us to import their legacy data, which is available in shape files, CAD files, and coverage feature classes in the geodatabase as well. We will start by importing the shape file as a geodatabase feature class. All the files are available in 8648OT_02_Files, which can be downloaded from the book's supporting files at www.packtpub.com. Copy the entire folder to your local drive before you carry on with the exercises.

Importing shape files

The shape files are in Esri's native file format, which was created a long time ago and is still being used heavily. Due to its simplicity, it has been adopted by a lot of GIS software. However, it is not designed for large datasets as it can introduce performance issues. In this section, we will import Belize shape files to the geodatabase. In order to do so, perform the following steps:

1. Open **ArcCatalog** and browse to your `Bestaurants` geodatabase.

2. Right-click on the geodatabase, point the cursor to **Import**, and then click on **Feature Class (single)...**.

3. In the new window, click on the folder icon next to the **Input Features** field to browse for the shape file we want to import to this location (`8648OT_02_Files\External_Data\Shape_files\Belize_Boundary.shp`).

4. Click on **OK** to select the location.

5. The output location should already be populated as your geodatabase. Finally, type in the name of the new imported feature class in the **Output Feature Class** field, name it `Belize_Boundary_Shape`, and then click on **OK** to start the importing process.

   This is illustrated in the following screenshot:

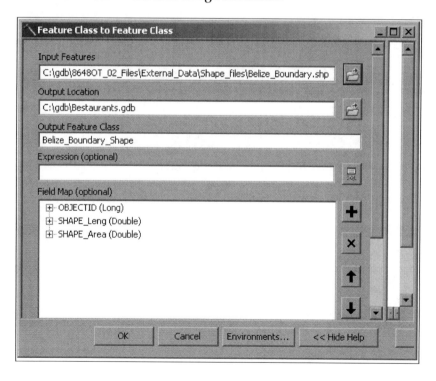

6. In order to see the progress of the importing process, point the cursor to **Geoprocessing** and then click on **Results**. You have now created a new feature class by importing shape files' data.

To-do
Test your new feature class by adding it to ArcMap.

Importing the CAD files

Now, we will import the CAD data, which was provided by the client, to our geodatabase. We need a special tool to do this. Perform the following steps to import a CAD file:

1. From the **Geoprocessing** menu, select **ArcToolbox**. This is a list of the rich tools that are helpful in authoring and working with geodatabases.

2. From the **ArcToolbox** window, expand **Conversion Tools** and then expand **To Geodatabase**.

3. Double-click on **CAD to Geodatabase**.

4. From the **CAD to Geodatabase** window, select **Input CAD Datasets** by browsing to the CAD files available in the following path: 8648OT_02_ Files\External_Data\CAD_files\Belize_CAD_Details.DWG.

5. Highlight Belize_CAD_Details.DWG by clicking on it once; then, click on **Add**.

6. In the **Output Geodatabase** field, browse to the Bestaurants geodatabase, and in the **Dataset** field, type the name of the new feature class as Belize_Boundary_CAD.

7. The spatial reference is already available in the CAD file and is imported, but in case it is not available, you can always set it later as we learned in *Chapter 1, Authoring Geodatabases*.

8. Click on **OK**, as shown in the following screenshot, to start the processing:

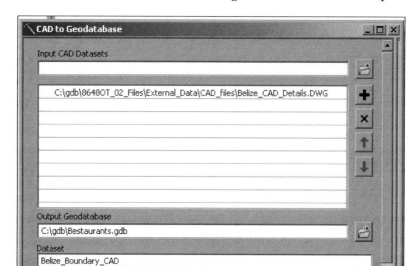

Note that the output is not a feature class but a feature dataset; a group of feature classes. We will discuss feature datasets in detail in the upcoming chapters.

A feature dataset is a dataset container for other geodatabase datasets. Feature datasets carry the properties (such as the spatial reference) that all child datasets inherit.

There are three feature classes, Polygon, Polyline, and BelizeBoundary. You can use the BelizeBoundary feature class and safely delete the other two. To delete a dataset from a geodatabase, right-click on the dataset and select **Delete**. You will be prompted whether you are sure you want to delete the object or not; choose **Yes**. Note that you cannot delete a dataset if it is already in use.

To-do

Compare Belize_Boundary_Shape and Belize_Boundary_CAD layers in ArcMap; are there any differences?

Importing coverage classes

Coverage is a geo-relational data model that stores vector data. It is a topological file whose boundaries are shared rather than repeated for individual features. Like the regular feature class, it contains both the spatial (location) and attribute (descriptive) data for geographic features. To import coverage files into a geodatabase, we can use the same tool we used while importing the shape files. In order to do so, perform the following steps:

1. From **ArcCatalog**, browse to geodatabase and right-click on the `Bestaurants` geodatabase.

2. Point the cursor to **Import** and click on **Feature Class (Single)**.

3. In the **Input Features** field, browse to the coverage feature class in the following path: `8648OT_02_Files\External_Data\Coverage_files\belize_shape\region.belize_shape`.

4. As shown in the following screenshot, type `Belize_Boundary_Coverage` in the **Output Feature Class** field.

5. Click on **OK** to create the feature class as shown in the following screenshot:

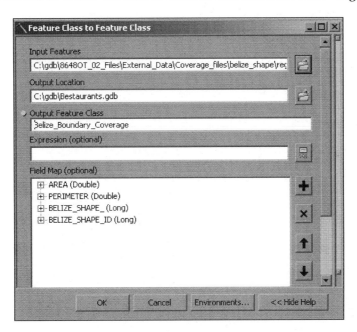

Summary

This chapter was lengthy and full of practical exercises. You have acquired new skills and tools that will allow you to do more on the geodatabase. You added new attributes, worked with domains and subtypes, and even created a relationship class that links multiple datasets together. You were able to create annotation classes that are useful for labeling maps. Finally, you learned how to import and convert other data files into your geodatabase and make them consistent in a single spatial reference so that you have a single geodatabase to manage, which will have all your data. So far, we have been creating datasets without paying attention to efficiency and optimization factors.

In the next chapter, we will discuss best practices for modeling the geodatabase in order to achieve an optimal and consistent design.

3
Modeling Geodatabases

In the previous chapter, we managed to complete a geodatabase, create feature classes, add attributes, work with domains, and so much more. However, it was a quick and rough design, not very efficient. We also had multiple feature classes which are almost identical. They have some differences, but they share a lot of attributes. You may imagine that if I ask you to delete an attribute in your geodatabase or change its size, you will have to do it in all these feature classes. We had to repeat a lot of steps and duplicate fields between the different feature classes, and that is because we didn't spend time on designing a proper model for our geodatabase.

Modeling geodatabases is important; it allows you to identify the weak points in your geodatabase design before implementing it physically. The moment you commit to a design and start populating your geodatabase, it becomes expensive to modify the schema. In this chapter, we will work on remodeling the `Bestaurant` geodatabase by creating an entity relationship diagram, a powerful modeling tool.

 An entity relationship diagram is a modeling tool for designing a database. It illustrates the different entities in a database and the relationships between them.

The entity relationship diagram for Bestaurants

A consultant was hired for the Bestaurants project to advise on the newly created geodatabase. After taking a look at the geodatabase, the consultant found it a bit difficult to assess the design by looking at the physical geodatabase. So, she suggested that we create an entity relationship diagram in order to visualize the design better and find the bottlenecks, if any.

The flaws in the current geodatabase

We will start by laying out the current entity relationship diagram as the consultant suggested. This way, we can identify the inefficiencies and flaws in the current model. There are a lot of tools available that enable you to do database modeling such as Microsoft Visio and ArcgoUML. I'm using an online tool called Gliffy for designing and modeling geodatabases. You can access it for free without creating an account at www.gliffy.com. You don't have to do the modeling part in this chapter; however, it is recommended that you model your design, even just on paper, before actually implementing it.

A dataset is modeled in a rectangular shape, with the name of the dataset in the header and the attributes added beneath it, each with their own type as follows (note how the OBJECTID attribute is bold and underlined, which indicates a primary key):

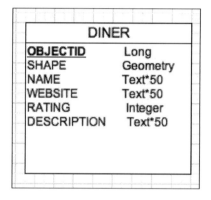

The relationship is modeled as a line between the two datasets, and the primary keys are highlighted in bold. Hence, if we model our current geodatabase, we should have something similar to the following figure:

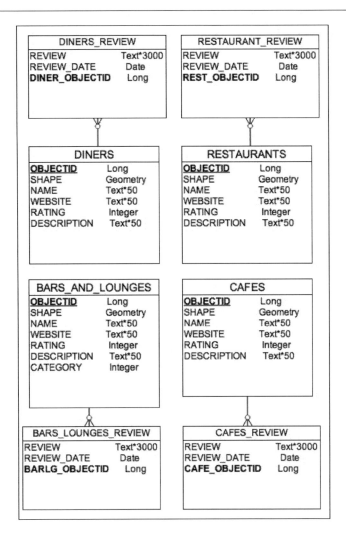

Now that we have our entity relationship diagram, the consultant is ready to start working. She first made a note of how attributes are duplicated between all the feature classes. In case we need to add a new attribute or delete an existing one, we should make sure that this change is reflected across all the geodatabase datasets to maintain data integrity. She also mentioned that querying would be more difficult with this model as you have to hit many tables to search for a record. Finally, the consultant pointed out that we have so many tables in our design because of unnecessary relationships. In the upcoming sections, we will learn how to remodel this design for more efficiency and less maintenance.

The proposed geodatabase model

So, we have some work to be done here. This geodatabase will work, but it will cost us a lot in the future in terms of maintenance. We can simplify this model by pruning a few feature classes from our geodatabase. Note that our four feature classes, `Restaurants`, `Diners`, `Bars and Lounges`, and `Cafes`, share something in common. They are all places where you can eat and drink, and all of these have a point type geometry as we have seen in *Chapter 1, Authoring Geodatabases*. So, we will start by merging all of them into a single feature class; let's call it `Food_and_Drinks`. Next, we will add the shared attributes, which, not surprisingly, are common between all four feature classes as follows:

Wait! There's still something missing; how will you distinguish a restaurant from a diner? You need an extra attribute; this is a perfect example of a subtype. Let's add the subtype field and name it CATEGORY. Remember, it should be an integer so that we can assign it as a subtype later. Finally, we need to assign the relationship. Luckily, we have only one feature class, so only one related table is required to store the reviews. We will call it `Venue_Reviews`. The modified model should look like the following figure:

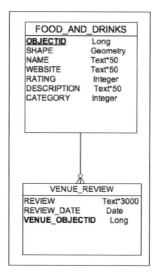

This is a much simpler design, and it will be much easier to create and maintain as well. Before the consultant left the meeting, she threw in another question: "What if tourists want to look at some pictures of the restaurant or diner?"

As you read the question, you may have figured out the solution to that. We can add a picture attribute so that we can add a single picture for a given venue. A second solution might be to create a related table so that we can add multiple pictures for a single venue. The second solution is better because you will have the luxury to add multiple photos for a given restaurant, including pictures of popular meals, the design of the venue, and so on. So, let's update our final design to accommodate the change as follows:

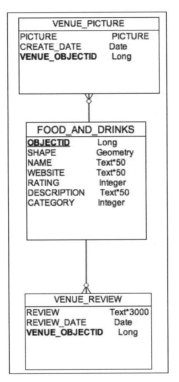

The concept of adding a picture, video, or file, for that matter, is called geodatabase attachment. This is a built-in option in ArcGIS that creates all the necessary related tables, which we will see and work on in the upcoming sections.

 Geodatabase attachment is a new feature in ArcGIS, which allows you to attach files to an existing dataset and store the files in a binary format. This, in turn, affects the size of the geodatabase depending on the attached objects.

Implementing the proposed model

We have a new model, so we need to create a new geodatabase. Let's keep our existing Bestaurants geodatabase and call the new one Bestaurants_new.

Authoring the geodatabase

To create the geodatabase, open **ArcCatalog**, browse to c:\gdb, and create a Bestaurants_new file geodatabase (refer to *Chapter 1, Authoring Geodatabases*, in case you have forgot how to do this). We need to create the RATING_SYSTEM domain. Right-click on the new geodatabase and select **Properties**, and then activate the **Domain** tab. We have done this previously in *Chapter 2, Working with Geodatabase Datasets*. The following screenshot will remind you how to create the domain:

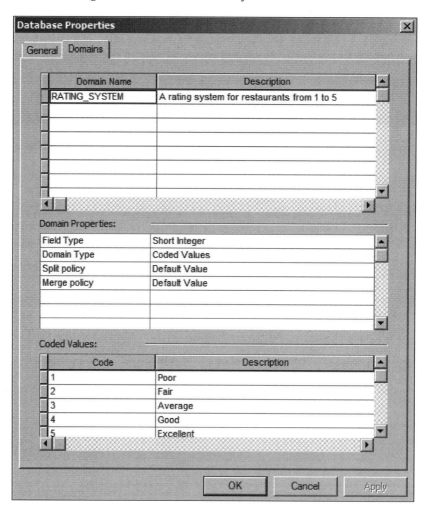

Creating geodatabase datasets

Next, we need to create the `Food_and_Drinks` feature class and then create the relationship. Right-click on the `Restaurants_new` geodatabase, point the cursor to **New**, and then select **Feature Class**. Name it `Food_and_Drinks`. Put a proper readable alias name; make sure that it is a point geometry and click on **Next**. In this form, we will select the spatial reference. If you don't remember what the spatial reference we selected before was, don't worry, you don't have to write it down and browse through the hundreds of spatial references. You can always import a spatial reference from an existing dataset (our old `Restaurant` geodatabase that you created in *Chapter 1, Authoring Geodatabases*), as illustrated in the following screenshot:

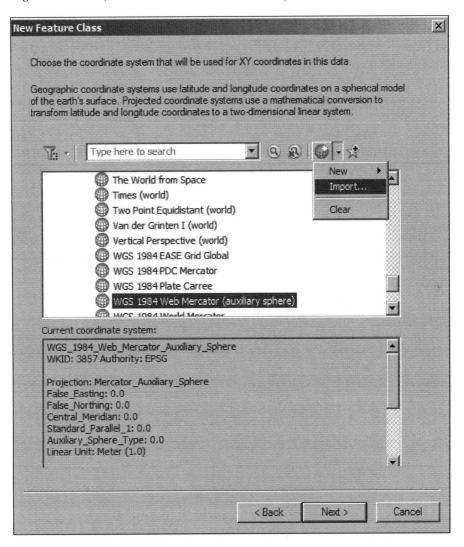

Keep the default values until you reach the **Attributes** page. Click on **Import...** so that you can import the attributes from an existing dataset. Browse to the old geodatabase and select the **Diners** feature class; then, click on **Add....** This will import all the attributes you need; we still need to go through each attribute and update the alias name to a proper name. We also need to add the CATEGORY subtype field of the type **Short Integer** as explained in the following screenshot:

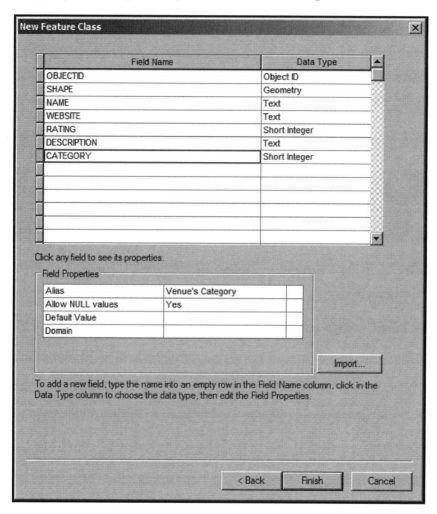

Next, we need to create the venue's review table for the relationship (refer to *Chapter 2*, *Working with Geodatabase Datasets*, in order to follow the steps). Right-click on the geodatabase and point the cursor to **New**. Then, select **Table**. Name it VENUES_REVIEW; keep the default parameters until you reach the attributes page where you will add the attributes shown in the following screenshot (don't forget to set plenty of text length for the REVIEW attribute):

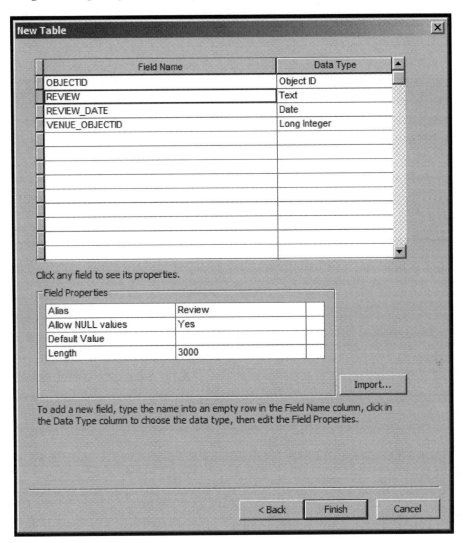

Now that we have created the table and the feature class, we need to join the two as we learned in the previous chapter. Create a new simple relationship class with backward messaging. Link the `Food_and_Drinks` feature class to the `VENUES_REVIEW` table. Your new geodatabase should look similar to what is shown in the following screenshot (refer to *Chapter 2*, *Working with Geodatabase Datasets*, for steps on how to create a relationship class):

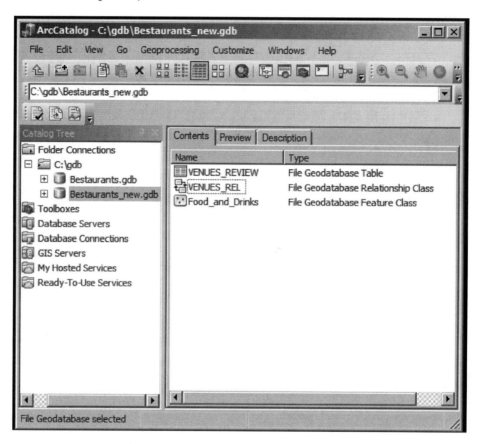

Assigning domains to the feature class

In the *Authoring the geodatabase* section, we created the `RATING_SYSTEM` domain. Now, we need to assign it to our `RATING` field. We have done this before; refer to the *Domains* section of *Chapter 2*, *Working with Geodatabase Datasets*, to repeat the steps.

Adding subtypes to the new feature class

We need subtypes to differentiate between the different types of restaurants.
To add subtypes, perform the following steps:

1. Open **ArcCatalog** and browse to your Bestaurants_new geodatabase.

2. Right-click on the **Food_and_Drinks** feature class and select **Properties**.

3. Activate the **Subtype Field** tab and select **CATEGORY** as the subtype field.

4. Add the subtypes, as shown in the following screenshot, and select
    Restaurant as your default subtype:

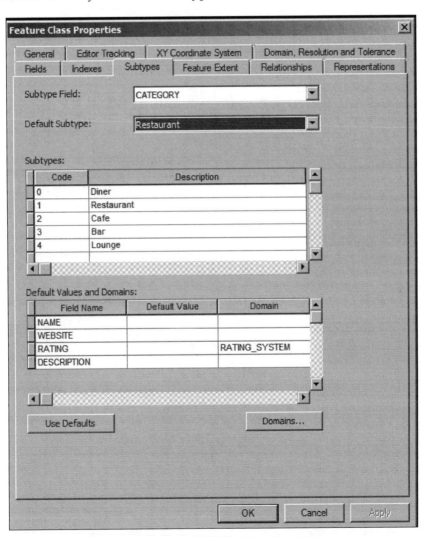

You may have noticed that what was previously a feature class is now being mapped as a subtype in our new model. This is interesting because we have pruned a number of feature classes and we are down to only one feature class. This will prove useful in *Chapter 4, Optimizing Geodatabases*, where we will learn techniques to optimize our feature classes. With this model, it will be easier and more convenient to apply configurations and optimizations mechanisms on a single feature class rather than on multiple ones.

Enabling attachments in the feature class

At the last minute, the consultant threw in another requirement, which was to add pictures to the venues. We will do something even better; we will allow any type of attachment, including pictures, videos, and even documents.

To enable the attachment on the feature class, perform the following steps:

1. Open **ArcCatalog** and browse to the new geodatabase.
2. Right-click on the **Food_and_Drinks** feature class, point the cursor to **Manage**, and then select **Create Attachments**, as shown in the following screenshot:

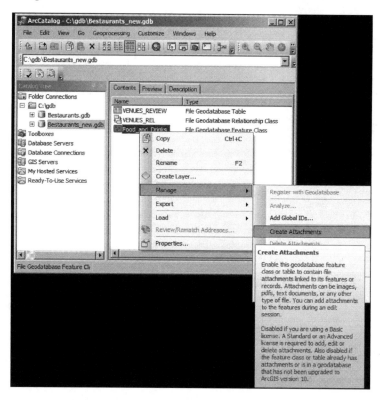

This feature is only available in the ArcEditor (standard) and ArcInfo (advanced) licenses; you cannot enable attachments on a basic ArcGIS license.

The last action threw in a couple of datasets and created the relationship, as you can see in the following screenshot. Take your time and explore these relationship classes:

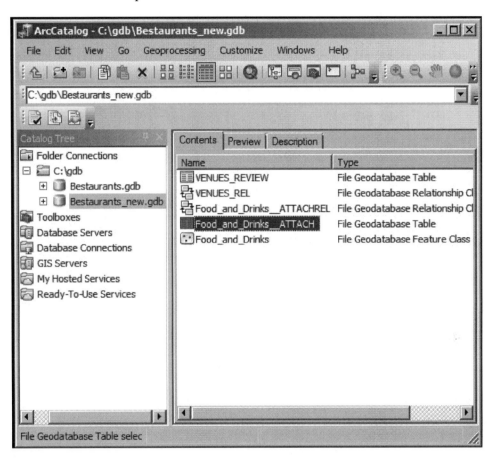

Testing the new geodatabase in ArcMap

Our new geodatabase is ready; it is time to put it to the test. Open `Belize_Basemap_new.mxd`. You can find it in the supporting files for this chapter, `8648OT_03_Files`, which can be downloaded from `www.packtpub.com`. Add the `Food_and_Drinks` feature class and set a proper symbology for each subtype, as we learned in *Chapter 2, Working with Geodatabase Datasets*. Start editing; let's add a lounge next to Water Lane street. If you can't find Water Lane street on the map, you can add it anywhere. Populate the new feature with the following attributes and any two reviews as shown in the following screenshot (refer to the *Working with object tables and relations* section of *Chapter 2, Working with Geodatabase Datasets*, to learn how to create related tables):

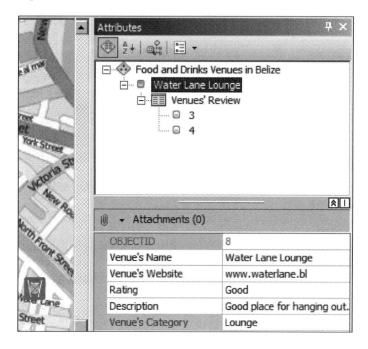

Now, it's time to test our new attachment option by adding a picture to our **Water Lane Lounge**. Can you see an attachment icon of a paperclip in the previous screenshot? Click on it to open **Attachment Manager**. In the **Attachments** dialog, click on **Add...** and browse to the `Water_Lane.jpeg` picture in `8648OT_03_Files`, as shown in the following screenshot:

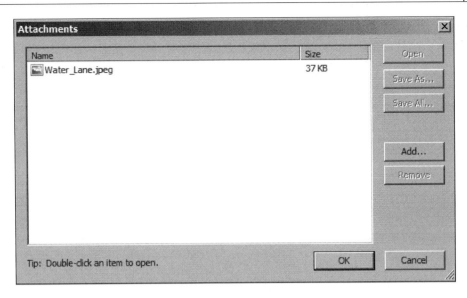

From the **Editor** toolbar, click on **Save Edits** to save the changes we have made on the geodatabase. Similarly, you can view the attachments for a given feature by using the identify tool in ArcMap. Activate the **Identify** tool and click on **Water Lane Lounge** in the map, and browse through the attributes, reviews, and attachments. Now, check the Food_and_Drinks feature class and explore how attachments are stored in the geodatabase.

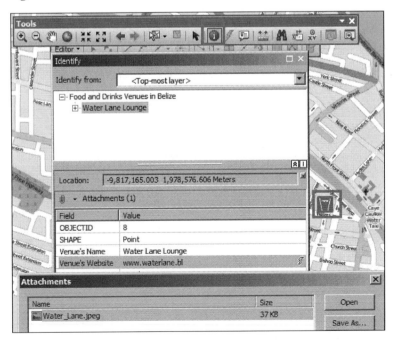

Use the **Editor** toolbar to add more restaurants, diners, bars, lounges, and cafes. Add some pictures and reviews to make your geodatabase rich.

Summary

In this chapter, you learned how to model the geodatabase. Using your newly acquired skills, you redesigned your model and simplified your geodatabase. You learned how to enable attachments on a feature class in order to allow attaching files for individual features. You also added new subtypes, reassigned the domains, and tested all this by the end of the chapter. In the next chapter, we will take the geodatabase to the next level by optimizing it to run effectively.

4
Optimizing Geodatabases

Modeling the geodatabase in the previous chapter helped produce a cleaner schema and reduced future maintenance costs. It was a necessary step to ensure a proper design, which in turn contributed directly to optimizing the geodatabase. As the geodatabase gets populated with features, its performance will naturally decline. The more features you have, the greater time the geodatabase takes to execute a query. That is why, in this chapter, you will be equipped with some new tools to help you tune the geodatabase to perform at its best. Some tools will be used only at the time of creating the geodatabase, while you will need to run the others frequently.

This chapter will run you through three themes. First, we will learn about indexing feature classes and how this can help boost querying. Second, we will introduce the concept of compressing, where we will learn how this can potentially reduce the size of the geodatabase. Finally, we will learn how compacting works and help speed up queries for a frequently edited geodatabase.

Indexing is a feature that helps speed up data retrieval for an attribute or a collection of attributes in a database table.

Compressing is a process by which the duplicated data in geodatabase datasets are simplified to decrease their size.

Compacting is a process by which a frequently edited geodatabase is cleaned from unused and orphan records.

Geodatabase indexing

Indexing is the de facto optimization standard for databases. It is a very powerful and effective tool that can help speed up the retrieval of records. Without indexing, a table is scanned entirely to retrieve a particular record. So, if we have a dataset with n records, the worst-case scenario is that the record we are trying to locate is the last record in that table, and thus we need to search through n records in order to reach it. Imagine a feature class with a million features, and the time taken to visit each feature is 1 millisecond; this means we need 17 minutes to scan the entire dataset. Of course, the response time depends on the record you are looking for; if it is located at the beginning of the feature class, it will take less time to be located.

Attribute indexing

Take a look at the `Food_and_Drinks` feature class in the following table. You can find this updated geodatabase in the supporting files for this chapter in `86480T_04_Files`, which can be downloaded from `www.packtpub.com`.

OID	Venue's Name	Venue's Website	Rating	Description	Venue's Category
8	Water Lane Lounge	`www.waterlane.bl`	Good	On Water Lane Street	Lounge
9	Haulze Restaurant	`www.haulze.bl`	Good	Located on Haulze	Restaurant
10	Haulze Lounge	`www.haulzelounge.bl`	Fair	Located on Haulze	Lounge
11	George Price Cafe	`www.gp.bl`	Excellent	An excellent cafe	Cafe
12	Starbucks Cafe [GP]	`www.starbucks.bl`	Good	Located on Lopez	Cafe
13	Mercy's Bar	`www.mercys.bl`	Average	On Mercy's	Bar
14	Mercy's Lounge	`www.mercys.bl`	Average	On Mercy's	Lounge
15	Croton's	`www.croton.bl`	Excellent	Excellent diner	Diner
16	Fern Diner	`www.fern.bl`	Poor	Fern Diner	Diner
17	Antelope's	`www.antelepe.bl`	Excellent	On Antelope	Restaurant
18	Gordon's	`www.gordon.bl`	Good	Located on Gordon's	Lounge
19	Crown's Cafe	`www.crown.bl`	Average	Located on Crown's	Cafe
20	Starbucks Cafe	`www.starbucks.bl`	Excellent	At Crown's	Cafe
21	Coney's	`www.coneys.com`	Excellent	Located at Coney's	Restaurant
22	Amara's	`www.amara.bl`	Good	Located at Amara's	Restaurant
23	Faber's Bar	`www.fabers.bl`	Average	Located at Faber's	Bar
26	Balan's Diner	`www.balan.bl`	Excellent	Balan's Diner	Diner
27	Cousin's Cafe	`www.cousin.com`	Excellent	An excellent cafe	Cafe

Let's say you need to find Croton's diner on the map, and you type in Croton's and hit *Enter*. ArcMap, or whichever GIS client you are using, forwards the search query to the geodatabase, which consequently starts scanning the feature class to locate the feature. Without indexing, the feature class is scanned feature by feature on the `Venue's Name` column to match the search term `Croton's`, as shown in the following figure:

Food and Drinks		
OID	**Venue's Name**	
8	Water Lane Lounge	<--Miss---
9	Haulze Restaurant	<--Miss---
10	Haulze Lounge	<--Miss---
11	George Price Cafe	<--Miss---
12	Starbucks Cafe [GP]	<--Miss---
13	Mercy's Bar	<--Miss---
14	Mercy's Lounge	<--Miss---
15	Croton's	<—Found—
16	Fern Diner	
17	Antelope's	
...	...	

As you can see, it takes the geodatabase more time to scan through these records one by one. Indexing is pretty much similar to how you arrange your files alphabetically at your desk at work. To enable indexing, the geodatabase creates another structure for the attribute to be indexed. In this example, we will create an index for the `Venue's Name` column, which points all letters to their matching object IDs. So, when we search for Croton's, this time with indexing, the geodatabase looks through the index for the letter C and finds only four records to scan.

Luckily, Croton's is the first feature, as illustrated in the following figure:

Venue's Name Index	
OID	**Index**
17, 22	A
24	B
15, 19, 21, 25	C
16, 23	F
11, 18	G
9, 10	H
13, 14	M
12, 20	S
8	W

—Found—▷

Food and Drinks	
OID	**Venue's Name**
8	Water Lane Lounge
9	Haulze Restaurant
10	Haulze Lounge
11	George Price Cafe
12	Starbucks Cafe [GP]
13	Mercy's Bar
14	Mercy's Lounge
15	Croton's
16	Fern Diner
17	Antelope's
18	Gordon's
19	Crown's Cafe
20	Starbucks Cafe
21	Coney's
22	Amara's
23	Faber's Bar
24	Balan's Diner
25	Cousin's Cafe

Indexing works similarly with almost any field type, text, numbers, date, and even spatial data types such as the Esri shape geometry type. Indexes created on shape columns are called spatial indexes, which have the same concept as attribute indexes. Both of them shrink the query search domain to achieve greater performance.

A spatial index is an index that is used on spatial data type columns such as geometry. It allows the spatial query to be run on a subset grid instead of an entire geodatabase grid.

Adding an attribute index

Suppose your clients started to perform attribute queries on their geodatabase, and they asked you whether you could tune it for better performance. We will start by adding an attribute index. However, the question is, on which attribute shall we create an index? Usually, this question is answered while modeling the geodatabase, where indexes are added in the entity relationship diagram. Indexes are created on attributes that are frequently queried. In the `Bestaurants` geodatabase, the `Venue's` `Name` field is a good candidate to create an index for. To create an attribute index, perform the following steps:

1. Copy the geodatabase in `8648OT_04_Files\Geodatabase` to the `c:\gdb` folder. You can create a backup of your geodatabase if you want to.

2. Open **ArcCatalog**.

3. Browse to the new geodatabases from the **Catalog Tree** window.

4. Right-click on the **Food_and_Drinks** feature class and select **Properties...**.

5. In the **Feature Class Properties** dialog, select the **Indexes** tab.

6. The **Attribute Indexes** section shows the existing indexes on the feature class. As you can see, there is an **FDO_OBJECTID** index (the primary key), which is a very important index that cannot be removed. The geodatabase uses this index to uniquely identify each feature. When you click on **FDO_OBJECTID**, in the **Fields** section, you will see the field on which this index is created for, as shown in the following screenshot:

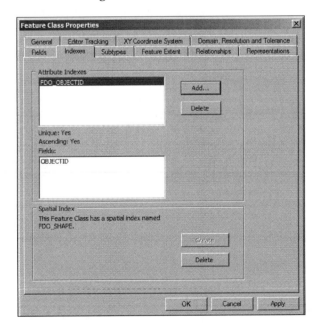

7. Click on **Add...** to add a new attribute index.

8. In the **Add Attribute Index** dialog, type in IND_NAME in the **Name** field. This is the index name.

9. From the **Fields available** list, select the **NAME** field, which is the Venue's Name column, and click on the right arrow icon to add it to the list, as you can see in the following screenshot:

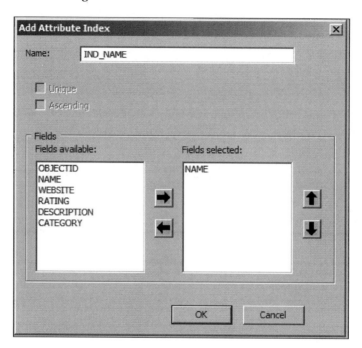

 The **Unique** and **Ascending** checkboxes are disabled by default for file geodatabases; however, they can be enabled for enterprise geodatabases depending on the underlying relational database system. This will be discussed in *Chapter 6, Enterprise Geodatabases*.

10. Click on **OK** to close the dialog to return to the indexes form.

11. You will see that the **IND_NAME** index has been created on the **NAME** field, and now all queries against the **NAME** field will be optimized. Click on **Apply** and then click on **OK** to close the dialog and return to **ArcCatalog**, as shown in the following screenshot:

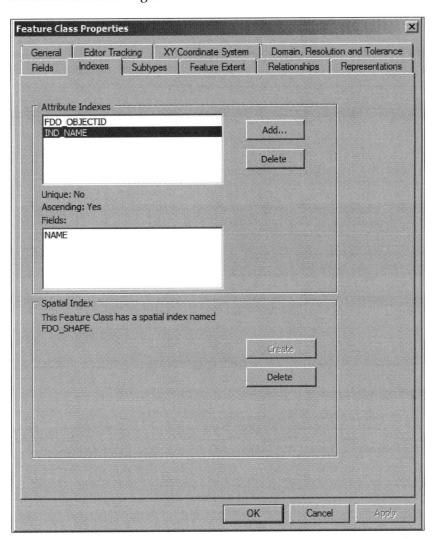

Spatial indexing

Spatial indexes work like attribute indexes, except they use square grids instead of records. Without a spatial index, retrieving restaurants in a given area takes more effort. This is because the geodatabase has to scan all the features to find out the ones that are in the given parameter. This is illustrated in the following figure. The square is the area we want to find all restaurants. Note how the scanning starts from left to right until a match is found; this takes a long time. The result will be features 22, 14, 16, 18, 17, and 15, as shown in the following figure:

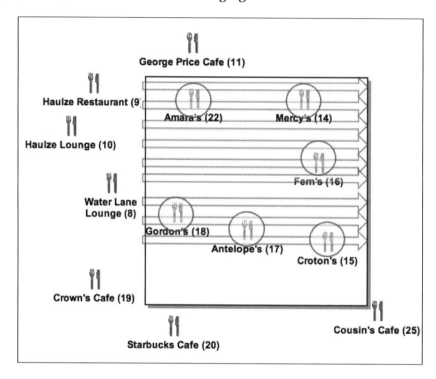

Spatial indexing creates small square grids in the entire feature class extent and updates the relationship between each grid and the features inside that grid. This information is stored in a separate table, which speeds up searching as shown in the following figure. Geodatabases simply scan the spatial index grid table. Those grids with no features are automatically skipped, which saves query execution time. We will get the same result, that is, 22, 14, 16, 18, 17, and 15, but much faster.

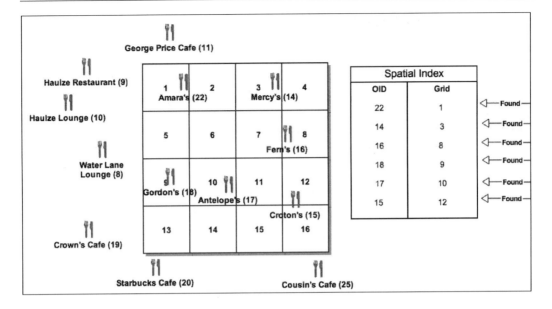

Adding a spatial index

When you create a feature class, a spatial index is automatically created and optimized for that feature class. At any time, you can drop and recreate the spatial index by performing the following steps:

1. Open **ArcCatalog** and browse to the Restaurants geodatabase.
2. Right-click on the **Food_and_Drinks** feature class and select **Properties...**.
3. Click on the **Indexes** tab.
4. In the **Spatial Index** section, click on **Delete** to delete the spatial index.
5. Click on **Create** if you want to create the spatial index again.
6. Close **ArcCatalog**.

 Deleting and recreating the spatial reference is a good exercise on a geodatabase that is frequently edited, as that will ensure consistency in spatial querying.

Using indexes effectively

Although indexing is a great tool for optimization, it can be harmful if implemented incorrectly. When you index a column, the geodatabase creates an additional hidden structure that needs to be managed and refreshed frequently. The more indexes you have, the more extra work the geodatabase has to endure to update those indexes. Indexes also slow down update operations such as INSERT, UPDATE, and DELETE, because the geodatabase has to change the indexes as well. More indexes mean that geodatabases need to update and, perhaps, even recreate those indexes. Avoid creating indexes on columns with very few distinct values such as rating and category because they often won't give you the performance you desire. It is good to create indexes on unique columns or nearly unique columns—indexes thrive on uniqueness and will always boost the performance of your geodatabase. You can calculate the percentage of indexing performance using the following formula:

$$ind(a) = \frac{d(a)}{n(a)} \cdot 100$$

In the preceding formula, *a* is the attribute to be indexed and *ind(a)* is the percentage of indexing efficiency; 100 percent being the maximum and 0 percent being the lowest. *d(a)* is the number of distinct values in the attribute column *a* and *n(a)* is the number of total values in *a*. Note that if *a* is a primary key, then *ind(a)* is 100 percent. This also explains why the RATING and CATEGORY fields score low on indexing performance in this formula.

Geodatabase compression

Compressing is an Esri feature that helps reduce the size of a file geodatabase by finding repetitive patterns in the database and grouping them together. This is a different concept than compacting, which we will also address later. For example, if you have your Food_and_Drinks feature class with 10 features, and all of them have the RATING field set to Good, compressing the feature class will count the Good values and add the number of occurrences as Good(10). When this feature class is accessed, the data is unpacked again and queried as desired. You might think that the processor needs to perform some work before querying and therefore, this might slow down the performance. However, with the advanced microprocessors and multithreading, this little extra work is barely noticeable.

Compressing a file geodatabase

It is important that you do not confuse the compressing of a file geodatabase with the compressing of an enterprise geodatabase (which is out of the scope for this book). Compressing a file geodatabase does not delete any data it maintains. It also prevents you from editing your file geodatabase. To compress a file geodatabase, perform the following steps:

1. Open **ArcCatalog**.

2. Browse and right-click on the file geodatabase, point the cursor to **Administration**, and then click on **Compress File Geodatabase**, as shown in the following screenshot:

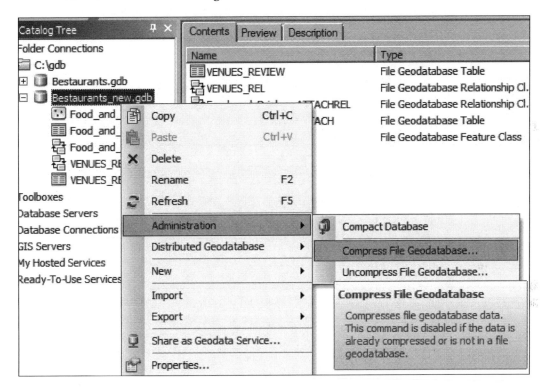

The compress operation can be lossless or lossy. Lossy compression was the only option available prior to ArcGIS 10.0 file geodatabases. In geodatabases that run on Versions 10 and higher, you have two options: lossy and lossless compression.

> Lossy compression is the process by which the content is compressed while losing some of its content. It is an irreversible operation.
>
> Lossless compression is compressing the content while preserving the data. It is a reversible operation.

3. In the **Compress File Geodatabase Data** dialog, make sure the **Lossless compression** checkbox is checked and click on **OK**, as shown in the following screenshot:

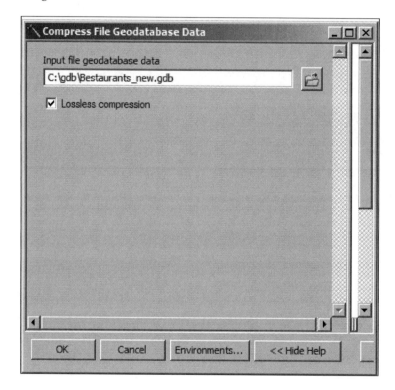

4. While compressed, the geodatabase is labeled as read only. This means you cannot perform any editing operation on the geodatabase. If you try to use ArcMap to edit, you will get the following message:

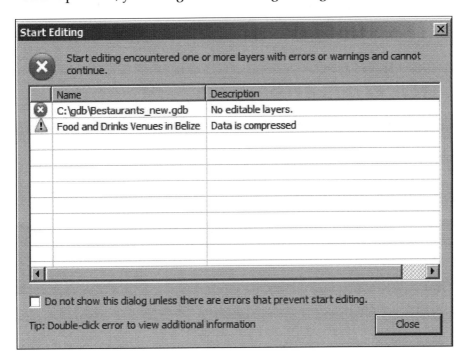

Using compression effectively

Compression can be used to save plenty of disk space, especially for geodatabases with a large number of features. If the geodatabase is mature enough and is not edited for a long time, it is healthy to use lossless compression to reduce its size.

 Before using compression, always create a backup of your file geodatabase. This is because compression can sometimes corrupt the geodatabase and render it inaccessible.

Compacting

The clients are happy with the new optimization techniques introduced in the geodatabase. However, they noticed a bit of performance decline after intense editing sessions, and they asked you whether this can be fixed. We can introduce the concept of compacting here. Like compression, compacting can reduce the geodatabase's size and potentially speed up queries. In the database world, this process is commonly known as vaccuming. However, compacting works differently as compared to compressing. Except for lossy compression, compression in general doesn't exactly get rid of any bytes. It merely packs them up by grouping redundant pieces, while compacting physically deletes and purges unneeded orphan records. We will demonstrate how compacting works, but we first need to understand what happens while editing the geodatabase.

Compacting a file geodatabase

It is easy to compact a file geodatabase; actually, it is recommended to compact a geodatabase after a heavy edit session. To compact a file geodatabase, perform the following steps:

1. Open **ArcCatalog** and browse to the Bestaurants geodatabase.

2. Right-click on the Bestaurants geodatabase, point the cursor to **Administration**, and then click on **Compact Geodatabase**, as shown in the following screenshot:

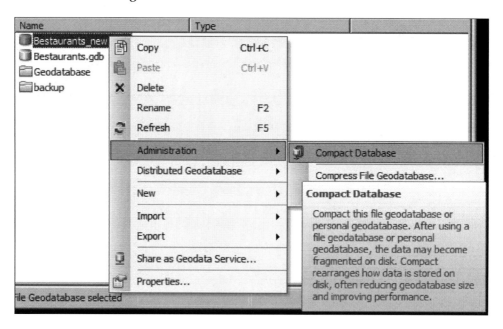

3. Your mouse will change to an hour glass and will return to be a normal cursor once compacting finishes.

Compacting is only valid for personal and file geodatabases. Enterprise geodatabases use versioning to perform editing, which has its own optimization techniques. We will discuss how to install an Enterprise geodatabase from scratch in *Chapter 6, Enterprise Geodatabases*.

Using compacting effectively

In this section, we will discuss how compacting a geodatabase works. Compacting is only effective on a frequently edited geodatabase, so we will start by performing a few edits. The following figure shows our healthy Restaurants geodatabase; let's say that we will delete the objects from 9 to 14:

Food and Drinks	
OID	**Venue's Name**
8	Water Lane Lounge
9	Haulze Restaurant
10	Haulze Lounge
11	George Price Cafe
12	Starbucks Cafe [GP]
13	Mercy's Bar
14	Mercy's Lounge
15	Croton's
16	Fern Diner
17	Antelope's
18	Gordon's
19	Crown's Cafe
20	Starbucks Cafe
21	Coney's
22	Amara's
23	Faber's Bar
24	Balan's Diner
25	Cousin's Cafe

(Rows 9 through 14 are marked with "—Delete—▷")

Logically, you may think that these records are removed permanently, and the rest of the features will move up to take their place. However, this is not exactly what happens; these records are simply marked as deleted in the geodatabase. Imagine if the geodatabase shuffles all records after each delete operation; editing will be extremely inefficient. That is why the geodatabase only marks the records as deleted and discards these records from any future queries. So, what happens when you try to locate Croton's (object 14)? It just so happens that the geodatabase has to go through all these records anyway and skip through the ones marked as deleted. Although they are deleted, they are, in a way, slowing down the query. This is illustrated in the following figure:

	OID	Venue's Name
		Food and Drinks
Miss ▷	8	Water Lane Lounge
Skip ▷	9	Haulze Restaurant
Skip ▷	10	Haulze Lounge
Skip ▷	11	George Price Cafe
Skip ▷	12	Starbucks Cafe [GP]
Skip ▷	13	Mercy's Bar
Skip ▷	14	Mercy's Lounge
Found ▷	15	Croton's
	16	Fern Diner
	17	Antelope's
	18	Gordon's
	19	Crown's Cafe
	20	Starbucks Cafe
	21	Coney's
	22	Amara's
	23	Faber's Bar
	24	Balan's Diner
	25	Cousin's Cafe

So what exactly does compacting do? As you might have guessed, compacting permanently removes these records and any other orphan records that are not used or referenced by any other objects. This is why compacting relatively speeds up queries against file geodatabases. As you can see in the next figure, `Croton's` can be found much more efficiently with a compacted geodatabase:

	Food and Drinks	
	OID	**Venue's Name**
—Miss—▷	8	Water Lane Lounge
—Found—▷	15	Croton's
	16	Fern Diner
	17	Antelope's
	18	Gordon's
	19	Crown's Cafe
	20	Starbucks Cafe
	21	Coney's
	22	Amara's
	23	Faber's Bar
	24	Balan's Diner
	25	Cousin's Cafe

Compacting is similar to the concept of defragmentation on your operating system. While deleting files on your Windows or Mac, your files become fragmented on the disc and your hard drive has to work harder to seek them. The defragmentation process groups the fragmented-free gaps and brings the files near each other so that they are easier to find. Before defragmentation, the files can be recovered with third-party applications that scan for patterns in the hard drive. However, after defragmentation, there is no way to recover these files.

Summary

In this chapter, you have learned three new optimization techniques that can be performed to achieve optimal efficiency for file geodatabases. You worked with both spatial and attribute indexing, and you learned when to use each efficiently. You also learned that overusing indexing could cause a performance penalty if planned poorly. Then, you worked with compression, which helps drastically reduce the geodatabase size and save plenty of disk space. Finally, you learned how compacting can help speed up queries of a frequently edited geodatabase. The next chapter will discuss some scripting and programming techniques on how to manage and administer the geodatabase using the file geodatabase API.

5
Programming Geodatabases

During the course of this book, you have learned about the key tools to author, manage, and administer ArcGIS geodatabases. You have learned how to create a geodatabase, add datasets, create relationships, and much more. In the previous chapter, you learned some techniques that can be applied to the geodatabase to optimize and keep your geodatabase healthy. You might have noticed that running all these tools manually, especially in bulk mode, can be a hectic process. That is why Esri, the company that created ArcGIS, has made all these geodatabase functionalities available as geoprocessing tools. These tools can be combined and joined together to form other tools with different functionalities. They can also be called from various programming platforms such as Python to solve interesting problems, as we
will see later in this chapter.

> A geoprocessing tool is a component that accepts input parameters and produces an output by performing operations on a geodatabase.
>
> Python is a high-level programming language used for many applications. The simplicity, open source standard, and object-oriented architecture of the language is what makes it popular.

We will discuss two methods for programming geodatabases; the first one is Python scripting, which is considered the pillar scripting language for ArcGIS, and the second one is model builder, which is a very effective way to build models from existing geoprocessing tools.

> Model builder is a feature built on top of ArcGIS, which allows the user to combine multiple geoprocessing tools into a single logical model to perform a complicated task easily.

Using Python scripting

Due to the simplicity of Python, the 23-year-old scripting language has been widely used to build various applications. Python has also been embedded into other products as a way to extend its functionality. ArcGIS is one of these products that adopted Python for this purpose. In this section, we will learn about a basic Python script to call existing geoprocessing tools, and then we will use these scripts to create a small tool that automatically backs up our Bestaurant geodatabase on a daily basis.

 To learn more about advanced Python scripting techniques, you can visit www.Python.org.

You don't have to install Python for the upcoming exercises; if you have ArcGIS for Desktop 10.x, Python 2.7 is installed and configured and ready for use. Let's do some basic warm up exercises on Python before we start on the real work:

1. Click on the **Start** menu, expand the **ArcGIS** folder, expand **Python 2.7**, and then click on **IDLE (Python GUI)** to open the Python editor, as shown in the following screenshot:

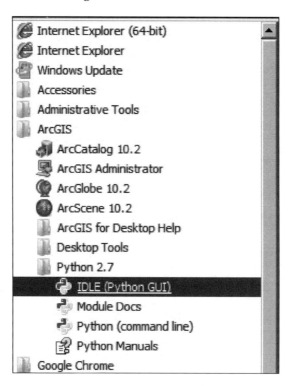

2. If you can't find it on the **Start** menu, you can access it by typing
`c:\Python27\ArcGIS10.2\Pythonw.exe "c:\Python27\ArcGIS10.2\Lib\`
`idlelib\idle.pyw"` in the run command. This is assuming you have ArcGIS
10.2 installed.

3. From the **Python Shell** window, point the cursor to **File** and then click on
New Window so that we can start working.

   We are going to write a simple script that accepts two integers, sums them,
   and prints the answer. I'm going to assume that you know some basic
   programming concepts such as variables and functions for this exercise.
   In the following example, we are going to build the script in small pieces,
   and then, when we're finished, we'll save and run the script.

4. Let's declare a variable, a, and assign it the value of 7, and we will declare
   another variable, b, and assign it the value of 13. Type the following code
   in the Python editor:

```
a = 7
b = 13
```

5. Then, we will declare a new variable, s, which will have the sum of a and b;
   you might have guessed how to write it:

```
a = 7
b = 13
s = a + b
```

6. This will sum a and b and save the answer in the s integer. We are not
   done still; we need to print this result. The `print` command allows us to
   print values and strings. Note that we have to convert s to a string if we are
   planning to concatenate it with a string. For this, we use the `str` command
   as follows:

```
a = 7
b = 13
s = a + b
print "The sum is " + str(s)
```

7. Before we save this file, we will add one last line. Python scripts execute fast,
   and you will barely be able to see the output before the script is terminated.
   So, we add a line to pause the script by asking the user to press any key. The
   input command asks the user for a value and stores it in a variable. It also
   pauses the script until a user takes an action. Go ahead and add the input
   statement as you can see in the following code segment:

```
a = 7
b = 13
s = a + b
print "The sum is " + str(s)
input ("Press any key to continue..")
```

8. We are now ready to save the file. From the **File** menu, click on **Save** and then browse to `c:\gdb`. Create a new folder called `scripts`, where we will be storing our scripts. Name the file `sum.py`; your file should look like the following screenshot:

```
sum.py - C:/gdb/scripts/sum.py                                    _ □ X
File  Edit  Format  Run  Options  Windows  Help

a = 7
b = 13
s = a + b
print "The sum is " + str(s)
input ("Press any key to continue..")




                                                            Ln: 5 Col: 0
```

9. It's time to test our script. Close this window and go to `c:\gdb\scripts`; then, double-click on the `sum.py` file. You will get the following result:

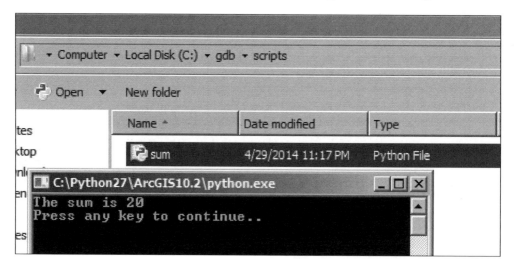

Let's modify the script so it asks the user for those numbers instead. For this, we need to use the `input` command.

Right-click on the `sum.py` file and click on **Edit with IDLE** to open the Python editor. Write the following code:

```
a = input("Enter the first number: ")
b = input("Enter the second number: ")
s = a + b
print "The sum is " + str(s)
input ("Press any key to continue..")
```

Save and run the code. Note that now you are prompted to enter the values of a and b instead of having them hardcoded in the script. We will be using the `input` command a lot to ask the user for parameters while working with our geodatabase.

 You can find this script along with other scripts that we will be using in the supporting files for this chapter under `86480T_05_Files\scripts`.

Creating a geodatabase

You now know how to create a basic Python script; let's now learn how to use Python to create our first file geodatabase programmatically. Esri has created a Python library called `arcpy` where all the geodatabase operations can be called. We need to reference this library using the `import` keyword in each script we write.

 The `arcpy` library is a Python library created by Esri that can be used to call ArcGIS geoprocessing tools from within Python.

Close any previously opened scripts and start a new Python script. We will start by importing the `arcpy` library and declaring a few variables for the geodatabase name and path. To start creating the file geodatabase, perform the following steps:

1. Write the following code into the Python editor. The `sgdb_path` variable is the path in which we want to create the geodatabase, while `sgdb_name` is the name of the geodatabase. Note that paths in Python are written with a common slash (/):

```
import arcpy
sgdb_path = "c:/gdb"
sgdb_name = "my_Python_gdb.gdb"
```

2. Executing the preceding code will not give you anything interesting just yet, as we still have not called the function responsible for creating our geodatabase. The `arcpy.CreateFileGDB_management` function accepts two parameters, the path and the name of the geodatabase. So, go ahead and write this down and pass in the two variables. Also, make sure to add a pause command at the end. Python is case sensitive, so you have to write it exactly as you see it in the following code snippet:

```
import arcpy
sgdb_path = "c:/gdb"
sgdb_name = "my_Python_gdb.gdb"
arcpy.CreateFileGDB_management(sgdb_path, sgdb_name)
input ("File created successfully, press any key to continue...")
```

3. Save the file as `create_gdb.py` in `c:\gdb\scripts` and run it. You can also run the script from the **Run** menu and then select **Run Module** or simply press *F5*.

4. Open **ArcCatalog** and browse to the `c:\gdb` folder. You should see the new file geodatabase, as shown in the following screenshot:

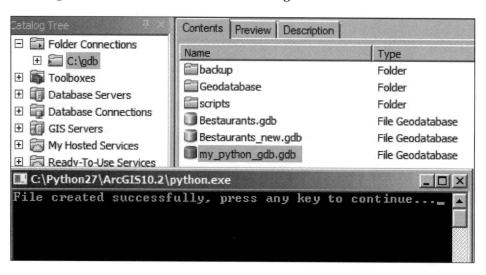

Creating a feature class

Python has helped us create a geodatabase; however, this geodatabase is empty, and we need more tools to help us populate it. For this, we will introduce the new `arcpy.CreateFeatureclass_management` command, which takes a minimum of three parameters: the full path of the geodatabase you want to create the feature class in, the name of the feature class, and the geometry type. To create a feature class, perform the following steps:

1. Open a new Python editor session and type the following lines of code:

   ```
   import arcpy
   sgdb_fullpath="c:/gdb/my_Python_gdb.gdb"
   sfc_name = "my_Python_featureclass"
   sgeometry = "POLYGON"
   arcpy.CreateFeatureclass_management(sgdb_fullpath,sfc_
   name,sgeometry)
   input ("Feature class created successfully, press any key to
   continue...")
   ```

2. Save the file as `create_fc.py` under the `scripts` folder and then run it.

3. Right-click on the geodatabase and click on **Refresh**. You should see your feature class created as well in the same geodatabase, as shown in the following screenshot:

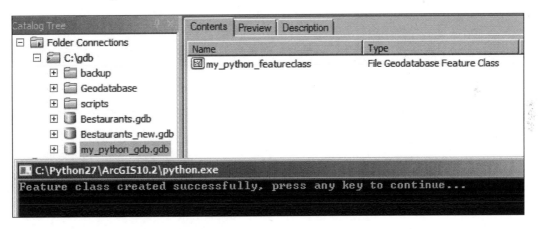

4. Close **ArcCatalog**.

All these operations, which require modifying the schema of the geodatabase, will throw an error if someone is already using the geodatabase. This is called a schema lock error.

Best practice

Python will throw a schema lock error if it is trying to change the schema of the geodatabase while it is in use by someone else. Always close all connections to the geodatabase before running your script.

Adding and deleting fields

Python has created a geodatabase and a feature class; however, this feature class has only the default attributes, the OBJECTID and SHAPE fields. It is time to learn how to let Python add fields to an existing feature class. This is done through the arcpy. CreateFileGDB_management command. The function takes a minimum of three parameters: the full path of the feature class, the name of the field to be added, and the type of the field. The full path to the feature class is basically the full path to the file geodatabase followed by a slash (\) and then the feature class name.

To add fields to a feature class, perform the following steps:

1. Close all other sessions, open a new Python editor session, and write the following code:

```
import arcpy
sfc_fullpath = "c:/gdb/my_Python_gdb.gdb/my_Python_featureclass"
sfield_name = "my_Python_field"
sfield_type = "LONG"
arcpy.AddField_management(sfc_fullpath, sfield_name, sfield_type)
input ("Field added successfully, press any key to continue..")
```

2. Save the file as add_field.py under the scripts folder and then run it.

3. To verify that the field is added, open **ArcCatalog** and browse to the geodatabase. Right-click on the feature class and click on **Properties**. As you can see in the following screenshot, the field was successfully created:

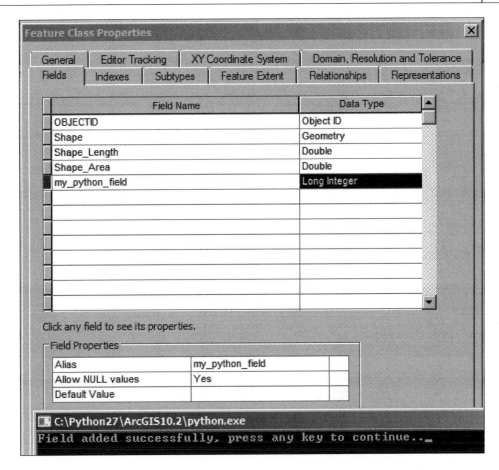

Similarly, you can delete a field with the `arcpy.DeleteField_management` command. This function takes the full path to the feature class and the name of the field to be deleted. To delete a field, type the following lines of code:

```
import arcpy
sfc_fullpath = "c:/gdb/my_Python_gdb.gdb/my_Python_featureclass"
sfield_name = "my_Python_field"
arcpy.DeleteField_management(sfc_fullpath, sfield_name)
input ("Field has been deleted successfully, press any key to
continue..")
```

Copying features

This one is an interesting geoprocessing tool and probably the most widely used one. It allows you to copy features from one feature class to another feature class. It accepts two parameters: the source feature class and the full path of the destination feature class. You do not need to create the new feature class as this tool creates it for you. Perform the following steps to copy features from one feature class to another feature class:

1. Open a new Python editor session and write the following code:

    ```python
    import arcpy
    sfc_source = "c:/gdb/my_Python_gdb.gdb/my_Python_featureclass"
    sfc_dest =  "c:/gdb/my_Python_gdb.gdb/my_Python_featureclass_copy"
    arcpy.CopyFeatures_management (sfc_source, sfc_dest)
    input ("Feature class copied successfully, press any key to
    continue...")
    ```

2. Save your file as `copy_features.py` under the `scripts` folder and then run your script.

3. You will see that the feature class is copied and a new feature class is automatically created, as shown in the following screenshot:

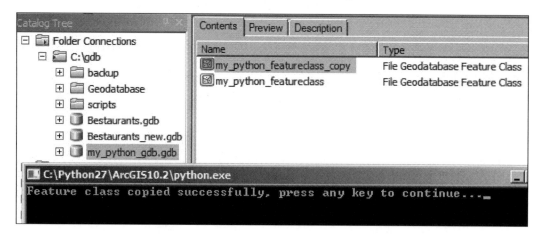

Backing up the Bestaurants_Web geodatabase

Earlier in this chapter, you acquired certain programming skills to help you work with geodatabases using Python. You will now use these skills to write a full script for a new assignment. Going back to our Belize client and the Bestaurants project, the geodatabase you created is growing and is becoming rich. It has reached a stage where it is ready to be published on the Web to be accessed by mobile. However, before doing that, the geodatabases have to be frequently backed up and some changes have to be made to the schema. The client asked you to create a new geodatabase called `Bestaurants_Web`, which is a lighter version of the geodatabase so it can be accessed swiftly. They suggested to remove some fields and the reviews. This geodatabase should be updated on a daily basis and a daily backup of the geodatabase should be kept, labeled by the date.

This is obviously a tedious job to be done manually. Therefore, we will use Python to help us in this assignment. According to the client, the `Bestaurants_Web` geodatabase should have only one feature class, named `Restaurants`, and no reviews or attachments. The following fields should be in the `Restaurant` table:

Field Name	Field Type
NAME	Text
WEBSITE	Integer
CATEGORY	Integer

We will break this assignment into three parts. First, we need to create the `Bestaurants_Web` geodatabase. Second, we need to copy the `Food_and_Drinks` feature class to the new geodatabase, and finally, we need to delete unwanted fields from the new feature class. The client also asked to create a daily backup of the `Bestaurants_Web` geodatabase, so our script should take care of that as well. This is an iterative process. We'll build the code piece by piece before saving and running the whole thing:

1. Create a new folder named `Web` under the `c:\gdb` folder.

2. Open a new Python editor session, save the file as `Web_Bestaurants.py` under the `scripts` folder, and let's start by creating a new `Bestaurants_Web` geodatabase. You should know how to create a file geodatabase by now:

```
import arcpy
sgdb_path = "c:/gdb/web"
sgdb_name = "Web_Bestaurants.gdb"
arcpy.CreateFileGDB_management(sgdb_path, sgdb_name)
```

> We didn't add the pause command because we will continue
> writing some code after that.

3. Save the file and continue writing. Next, we need to copy the `Food_and_
   Drinks` feature class from `Bestaurants` to the new geodatabase as follows:

```
import arcpy
sgdb_path = "c:/gdb/web"
sgdb_name = "Web_Bestaurants.gdb"
arcpy.CreateFileGDB_management(sgdb_path, sgdb_name)
sfc_source = "c:/gdb/Bestaurants_new.gdb/Food_and_Drinks"
sfc_dest = sgdb_path + "/" + sgdb_name + "/Restaurants"
arcpy.CopyFeatures_management (sfc_source, sfc_dest)
```

4. Next, we need to delete a few fields that are not necessary for the web
   version of the geodatabase. The RATING and DESCRIPTION fields should be
   deleted. We terminate the script with a message, letting the user know that
   the process has been completed. Add the following lines to your code:

```
import arcpy
sgdb_path = "c:/gdb/web"
sgdb_name = "Web_Bestaurants.gdb"
arcpy.CreateFileGDB_management(sgdb_path, sgdb_name)
sfc_source = "c:/gdb/Bestaurants_new.gdb/Food_and_Drinks"
sfc_dest = sgdb_path + "/" + sgdb_name + "/Restaurants"
#Copy features
arcpy.CopyFeatures_management (sfc_source, sfc_dest)
sfield_rating = "RATING"
sfield_desc = "DESCRIPTION"
arcpy.DeleteField_management(sfc_dest, sfield_rating)
arcpy.DeleteField_management(sfc_dest, sfield_desc)
input ("Web Bestaurants geodatabase created successfully, press
any key to continue.")
```

> We have used the # character. This indicates that the text
> after # will be treated as a comment.

5. Save the Python script and run it.

> Double-check that you have correct paths to avoid any
> possible errors in your Python script.

6. The output should look like the following screenshot after successfully running the script:

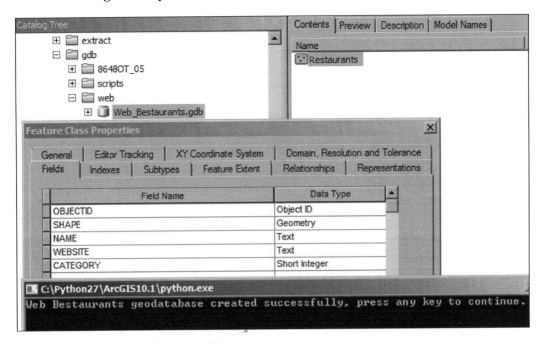

There is one step missing, the backup. In order to back up this geodatabase on a daily basis, we could rename the existing Web_Bestaurants geodatabase to Web_Bestaurants_TodayDate, and then run the script normally. Since the Web_Bestaurants geodatabase is no longer available (it has been renamed), the script will create a fresh geodatabase. We will need to add additional Python libraries, os and datetime. A Python library, such as arcpy, is a collection of useful methods that can be imported and used throughout the script. For instance, the os.rename method is used to rename a folder name, and datetime.date.today gives you the year, month, and day of the current date. Add the following lines to your code to do so:

1. Import the os and datetime libraries right after the arcpy library as follows:

```
import arcpy
import os
import datetime
sgdb_path = "c:/gdb/web"
sgdb_name = "Web_Bestaurants.gdb"
arcpy.CreateFileGDB_management(sgdb_path, sgdb_name)
sfc_source = "c:/gdb/Bestaurants_new.gdb/Food_and_Drinks"
sfc_dest = sgdb_path + "/" + sgdb_name + "/Restaurants"
#Copy features
```

```
arcpy.CopyFeatures_management (sfc_source, sfc_dest)
sfield_rating = "RATING"
sfield_desc = "DESCRIPTION"
arcpy.DeleteField_management(sfc_dest, sfield_rating)
arcpy.DeleteField_management(sfc_dest, sfield_desc)
input ("Web Bestaurants geodatabase created successfully, press
any key to continue.")
```

2. Write the following code snippet in your script after the `sgdb_name` line and before creating the file geodatabase:

```
import arcpy
import os
import datetime
sgdb_path = "c:/gdb/web"
sgdb_name = "Web_Bestaurants.gdb"
todaydate = str(datetime.date.today().year) + str(datetime.date.
today().month)  + str(datetime.date.today().day)
os.rename (sgdb_path + "/" + sgdb_name , sgdb_path + "/" + "Web_
Bestaurants" + todaydate + ".gdb")

arcpy.CreateFileGDB_management(sgdb_path, sgdb_name)
```

3. Finally, run the command and make sure it works.

4. This step is optional; we could add this script in Windows Scheduler for it to run. The following steps are necessary to do so:

    1. From the **Start** menu, type `taskschd.msc` to open up **Task Scheduler**.
    2. From the **Actions** panel, click on **Create Basic Task...** and type in the name of the task, `Web_Bestaurants_Backup`, and then click on **Next**.
    3. Select **Daily**, so the task runs on a daily basis. Click on **Next**.
    4. Select the time you want this task to run, leave it at **midnight**, and click on **Next**.
    5. Select **Start a program** and then click on **Next**. This way, we let Windows start our script.
    6. Browse to your `web_bestaurants.py` file.
    7. Click on **Finish**.

Note that if you have run the command multiple times, you will get an error. The reason is that the geodatabase is created on the first run, so when you try to run the script again it will create the geodatabase with the same name raising an error. To solve that you can delete the geodatabase before running the script.

As shown in the following screenshot, Windows will now run your script on a daily basis and create a copy of your Web_Bestaurants geodatabase:

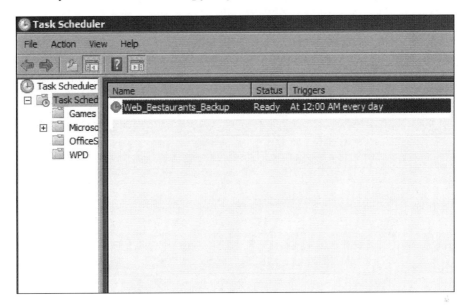

 Windows Scheduler is a service in Windows that allows the user to schedule applications to run at an event, such as at the startup of the computer or on a particular date or time.

Make sure to delete this scheduled task from your Windows after finishing the testing, else it will continue to run every day.

You can find a lot of the arcpy geoproessing commands at http://qr.net/packt_lag_dm. You can use them in a way that is similar to how we used the geoprocessing commands in this chapter. The Esri link also explains how to use them with a sample Python script.

A list of arcpy commands

This section includes a list of a lot of useful commands that you can use to work with geodatabases. This list has been compiled from www.esri.com.

Tool	Description	Python script example

Create File GDB	Creates file geodatabases	```# Create file geodatabase bestaurants.gdb in c:\gdb path.```
		```arcpy.CreateFileGDB_management```
		```(```
		```"c:/gdb",```
		```"bestaurants.gdb"```
		```)```

Create Feature class	Creates a feature class in an existing geodatabase	```# Creates the VENUE_BOUNDARY feature class of type polygon; this can be used to highlight the boundary of a given restaurant.```
		```arcpy.CreateFeatureclass_management```
		```(```
		```"c:/gdb/bestaurants.gdb",```
		```"Venue_Boundary",```
		```"POLYGON"```
		```)```
		
		```#Creates the VENUE_FENCE feature class of type polyline; this can be used to draw a fence around a restaurant if it has one.```
		```arcpy.CreateFeatureclass_management```
		```(```
		```"c:/gdb/bestaurants.gdb",```
		```"Venue_Fence",```
		```"POLYLINE"```
		```)```
		
		```#Creates a landmark feature class in the bestaurants geodatabase of type point. This feature class is used to indicate a landmark such as a building, a mall, or a train station.```
		```arcpy.CreateFeatureclass_management```
		```(```
		```"c:/gdb/bestaurants.gdb",```
		```"Landmark",```
		```"POINT"```
		```)```
		
		```#Creates the VENUE_BOUNDARY feature class of type polygon using Food_and_Drinks as a template feature class; this will import all fields and spatial references to this feature class.```
		
		```arcpy.CreateFeatureclass_management```
		```(```
		```"c:/gdb/bestaurants.gdb",```
		```"Venue_Boundary",```
		```"POLYGON"```
		```"c:/gdb/bestaurants.gdb/Food_and_Drinks",```
		```)```

Tool	Description	Python script example

Add Field	Adds a new field to an existing feature class	```#Adding a Number_Of_Tables long field which will have the number of tables in a given restaurant.```
		`arcpy.AddField_management`
		`(`
		`"c:/gdb/bestaurants.gdb/Food_and_Drinks",`
		`"Number_of_Tables",`
		`"LONG"`
		`)`
		
		`#Adding a HAS_WIFI text field which will have YES or NO as a value. This indicates whether this restaurant has Wi-Fi or not.`
		`arcpy.AddField_management`
		`(`
		`"c:/gdb/bestaurants.gdb/Food_and_Drinks",`
		`"Has_WIFI",`
		`"TEXT"`
		`)`
		
		`#Adding a CREATIONDATE field of type date, which will have the date on which this feature has been added or when this restaurant has been opened.`
		`arcpy.AddField_management`
		`(`
		`"c:/gdb/bestaurants.gdb/Food_and_Drinks",`
		`"CreationDate",`
		`"DATE"`
		`)`

Delete Field	Deletes an existing field from a feature class	`#Delete the HAS_WIFI field.`
		`arcpy.DeleteField_management`
		`(`
		`"c:/gdb/bestaurants.gdb/my_point_featureclass",`
		`"Has_WIFI"`
		`)`

Copy Features	Copies features from one feature class to another	`#Copy all features in the feature class Food_and_Drinks from an existing geodatabase to another existing geodatabase. This tool will automatically create a new feature class.`
		
		`arcpy.CopyFeatures_management`
		`(`
		`"c:/gdb/bestaurants_old.gdb/Food_and_Drinks",`
		`"c:/gdb/bestaurants_new.gdb/Food_and_Drinks"`
		`)`

Tool	Description	Python script example

Calculate Field	Fills a field with values based on a formula	```#Populates the CreateDate field in the food_and_drinks feature class with today's date.```
		```import datetime```
		```d = datetime.date.today()```
		```arcpy.CalculateField_management```
		```(```
		```"c:/gdb/bestaurants.gdb/Food_and_Drinks",```
		```"CreationDate",```
		```"'" + str(d) + "'",```
		```"PYTHON"```
		```)```

Compact	Compacts a personal or file geodatabase	```#Compacts the geodatabase located on c:\gdb\bestaurants.gdb.```
		```arcpy.Compact_management```
		```(```
		```"c:/gdb/bestaurants.gdb"```
		```)```

Compress	Compresses a file geodatabase	```#Compresses the geodatabase located on c:\gdb\bestaurants.gdb.```
		
		```arcpy.CompressFileGeodatabaseData_management```
		```(```
		```"c:/gdb/bestaurants.gdb"```
		```)```

Uncompress	Uncompresses a file geodatabase that is already compressed	```#Uncompresses the geodatabase located on c:\gdb\bestaurants.gdb; must be already compressed to be successful.```
		```arcpy.UncompressFileGeodatabaseData_management```
		```(```
		```"c:/gdb/bestaurants.gdb"```
		```)```

Using the model builder

Besides Python scripting, the model builder is a nice way to aggregate multiple geoprocessing tools without the need to have programming skills. If you found it difficult to write Python scripts, you can always use the model builder to create interesting models. In this section, we will use the model builder to build a sample model to create a file geodatabase and a feature class.

Creating a model

You can create a model from either ArcMap or ArcCatalog. To create a model, perform the following steps:

1. Create a folder in the `c:\gdb` folder and name it `myTools`.

2. Open **ArcCatalog**, point the cursor to the **Geoprocessing** menu, and then click on **ModelBuilder**.

 You can also use ArcMap to work with ArcToolbox.

3. Bring up the **ArcToolbox** window as well since we will use both. Keep both windows next to each other.

4. In the **ArcToolbox** window, expand **Data Management Tools** and **Workspace**, and then drag the **Create File GDB** tool to the **Model** window as illustrated in the following screenshot:

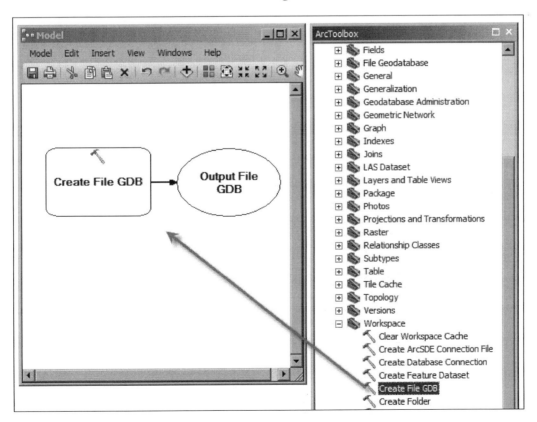

The `Create File GDB` tool is represented as a rounded rectangle, which indicates a geoprocessing tool with a single rounded oval, representing a variable. There are many variable types supported by the model builder. Some are native, such as `String`, and some are ArcGIS-related, such as `FeatureClass` and `Workspace`. In this case, the `Output File GDB` variable is of the `Workspace` type, which is essentially a geodatabase.

The `Create File GDB` tool accepts a number of variables that are not exposed by the model builder by default; we need to add these variables. The first one is the path where we want to create the geodatabase and the second variable is the name of the file geodatabase. To add an input parameter, right-click on the `Create File GDB` rectangle, point the cursor to **Make Variable**, then point the cursor to **From Parameter** and select the variable name. You will have a list of all possible input parameters as shown in the following screenshot:

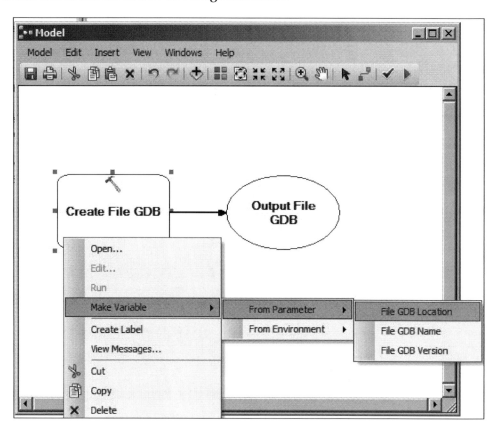

Similarly, add the **File GDB Location** and **File GDB Name** variables. Once you add the second one, they will be drawn on top of each other. Move them around so they don't overlap. These variables are still not exposed to the user as input. To do so, we need to make them a model parameter. Right-click on **File GDB Location** and then click on **Model Parameter**. The letter **P** will be displayed on that variable, which means that this variable is exposed as a parameter in the model interface. Make **File GDB Name** a model parameter as well, as shown in the following screenshot:

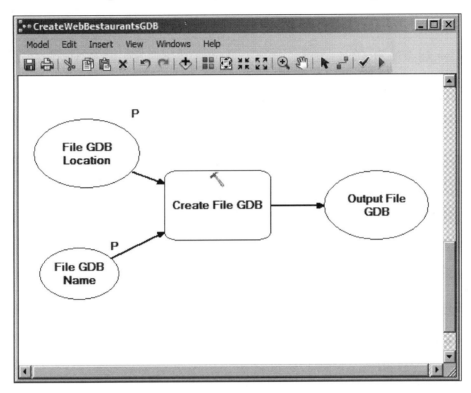

Now it is time to save the model before we add more tools. To save the model, perform the following steps:

1. Click on the **Model** menu and then click on **Save**.

2. Browse to `c:\gdb\MyTools` and click on the **New ToolBox** icon to create a new toolbox where we will be storing our model.

3. Name it Web_Bestaurants, as shown in the following screenshot (note that this is not our model, it is just a container that will contain our model):

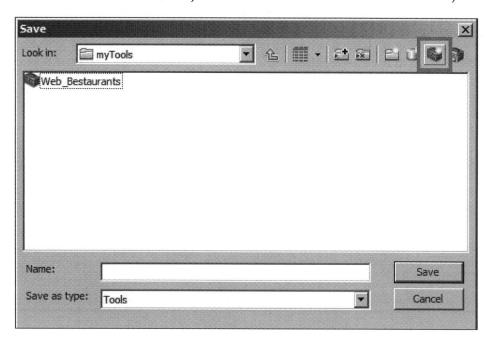

4. Double-click on the **Web_Bestaurants** toolbox to open it.

5. In the **Name** field, type CreateWebBestaurantsGDB, and then click on **Save** to save your model.

6. Close the model.

7. To open the model from the **Catalog Tree** window, browse to the **CreateWebBestaurantsGDB** model in c:\gdb\MyTools and then right-click on it and click on **Edit...**, as shown in the following screenshot:

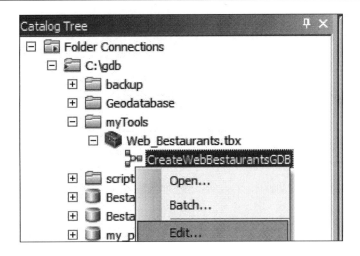

8. Close the model but keep **ArcCatalog** opened.

Creating a feature class

To create a feature class, we need to specify a few parameters such as the feature class name and geodatabase location. We previously created a geodatabase; we will now learn how to link that output and serve it as an input to our new tool. To do so, perform the following steps:

1. Browse to the **Create Feature Class** tool from **ArcToolbox**; you can find it under **Data Management Tools | Feature Class**.

2. Drag **Create Feature Class** to the model.

3. Add **Feature Class Name** as a model parameter for the **Create Feature Class** tool, as explained previously.

4. Use the **Connect** tool in the model builder to connect **Output File GDB** to the **Feature Class Location** variable in the **Create Feature Class** tool, as illustrated in the following screenshot:

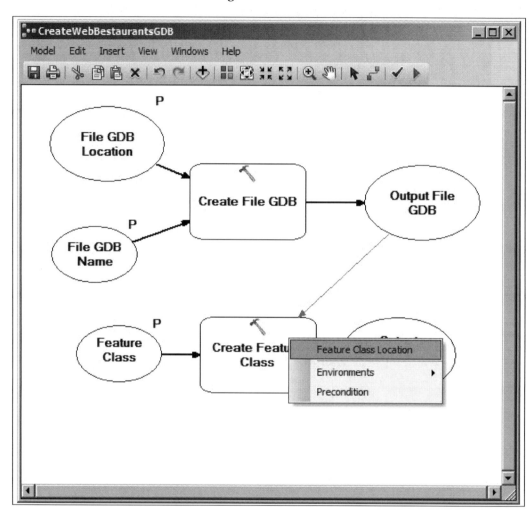

5. Save the model and close it.

Running the model

Finally, we have completed our simple model, and now it is time to test it. To run a model, perform the following steps:

1. Browse to **c:\gdb\myTools\Web_Bestaurants.tbx** from the **Catalog Tree** window and double-click on **CreateWebBestaurantsGDB**. You will get a dialog box with three kinds of input. Remember that these are our model parameter variables in the model: **File GDB Location**, **File GDB Name**, and **Feature Class Name**.

2. In the **File GDB Name** field, type `my_model_gdb`.

3. Set the **File GDB Location** field to **c:\gdb**.

4. Finally, type `my_model_fc` in the **Feature Class Name** field, as illustrated in the following screenshot:

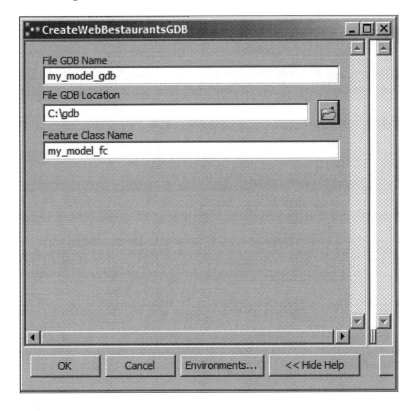

5. Click on **OK**.

After the process is completed, you can see that your geodatabase and feature class are created. You can start mashing up multiple tools to create fascinating customized geodatabase tools.

Summary

In this chapter, we discussed some programming flavors. You perceived working with geodatabases from a completely different angle. The chapter demonstrates two methods for programming geodatabases, Python and model builder. Python took the lion's share in this chapter; at first, you learned how to work with basic Python scripting. Then, you were introduced to the `arcpy` module built by Esri, which allows Python to tap into the power of ArcGIS and do much more. You dove deep into Python by solving a real-world problem from the ground up using Python. Then, you learned about the model builder and how you can combine and mash up multiple geoprocessing tools to create more sophisticated tools. Unlike Python, the model builder requires no programming skills to work on, which makes it desirable for many users.

In the next chapter, we will discuss how to install, configure, and administer an enterprise geodatabase with Microsoft SQL Server Express from scratch. Enterprise geodatabases are powerful, support multiusers, and are recommended for a large number of users.

6

Enterprise Geodatabases

In the previous chapters, we worked with file geodatabases. File geodatabases are easy to use, convenient, and portable. You can work with them in a completely disconnected environment. You can also transfer a file geodatabase with a map document in a thumb drive, work on it, and make changes. For personal use and work, file geodatabases work great.

However, they cannot fit your solution every time. There are cases where you need multiple users to access and edit data. You might need to view the geographic data from another computer on the network without actually copying the data to that machine. Then there is, of course, the security and integrity of the data. There is no access control on a file geodatabase; anyone with a hold on the file can do whatever they want with it. You don't know who deleted, edited, or modified the schema on a file geodatabase. When you find yourself in this situation, this is when you are in need of an enterprise geodatabase.

Although I wouldn't be able to do justice to enterprise geodatabases in a single chapter, I will try my best to cover the vital points of this interesting topic. This topic alone requires a dedicated book just to write about all the benefits, configurations, when and when not to use them, and best practices that can be applied during the implementation of enterprise geodatabases. In this chapter, we will install, configure, and work with a complete enterprise geodatabase using Microsoft SQL Server Express 2012 SP1.

 An enterprise geodatabase is a geodatabase that is built and configured on top of a powerful relational database management system. These geodatabases are designed for multiple users operating simultaneously over a network.

The benefits of the enterprise geodatabase

Although an enterprise geodatabase requires you to invest in the management and administration, the benefits can be highly rewarding. Enterprise geodatabases are built on top of relational database management systems such as Microsoft SQL Server, Oracle, and DB2. These systems are powerful and are wired to sustain constant editing and multiple accesses. With enterprise geodatabases, you can do the following tasks:

- Set up access control
- Build a centralized geodatabase which can be accessed from multiple terminals
- Restrict certain users from viewing a feature class or table
- Restrict certain users from editing a feature class or table
- Restrict users from changing the geodatabase schema
- Edit tracking to know who added a new feature or edited an existing one

In the next section, we will start with the installation of Microsoft SQL Server Express 2012 Service Pack 1.

Setting up a Microsoft SQL Server Express geodatabase

SQL Server Express is a lightweight, free database management system that is provided by Microsoft. We are going to use it for our enterprise geodatabase. For the production environment, you will need something stronger than this database, such as SQL Server, Oracle, DB2, or PostgreSQL. For the purpose of demonstration, we will use SQL Server Express. It is a good test case as it's easy to set up and use, and since it's a Microsoft product, it integrates well with ArcGIS.

System requirements

Before we start, we will need a new machine to work on. This will be our geodatabase server. You can use the machine you are working on now, but I recommend that you use another machine to see the complete benefits of enterprise geodatabases. A virtual machine with 2 GB RAM, 50 GB of hard drive space, and either a 64-bit Windows 7 SP1 or Windows Server 2008 R2 SP1 or higher is recommended. I'm running on a 2 GB Windows Server 2008 R2 SP1 virtual machine. SQL Server Express also requires Microsoft .NET Framework 3.5 Service Pack 1; make sure it is installed on your machine before you proceed. The .NET Framework can be found in the supporting files under 8648OT_06_Files\installers or can be downloaded from http://www.microsoft.com/en-us/download/details.aspx?id=25150. You can also install the Application Server role if you have Windows Server 2008 R2 SP1 or higher, which installs the framework by default.

If you have a fresh machine, name it GDBSERVER; this is the name of my machine. However, you can pick any other name you want as long as you keep using it consistently.

 You will require an ArcGIS for Server license to start working on this chapter and to create an enterprise geodatabase. You can ask your local Esri distributor for a trial version.

Installing SQL Server Express

First, we will install the database software. You can find the SQLEXPRWT_x64_ENU.exe installer file in the 8648OT_06_Files\installers supporting files. The file can also be downloaded from http://qr.net/mssqlexpress. Click on **Download** then select the SQLEXPRWT_x64_ENU.exe file. This installer is for Microsoft SQL Server 2012 Service Pack 1 (SP1) Express. This is a large file (1 GB) as it has the database and the management tools.

If your computer fits the requirement, you will be prompted with the **SQL Server Installation Center** dialog. We are now in the installation stage; perform the following steps to install SQL Server Express:

1. Click on the **New SQL Server stand-alone installation or add features to an existing installation** link as shown in the following screenshot:

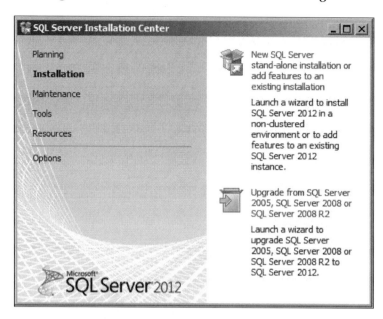

2. You will be prompted with the SQL Server 2012 setup licenses' terms and conditions. If you have the time, you can always read through the agreement.

3. After this, check the **I accept the license terms** checkbox and click on **Next**.

4. If you are prompted with the **Product Updates** page, uncheck the **Include SQL Server Product Updates** checkbox and click on **Next**. Note that you might not get this page when you are not connected to the Internet.

5. The setup will scan for existing products already installed on the system, and then it will commence installing the setup files. Wait until you get the **Feature Selection** form.

6. The setup will now ask you to select the features for your installation.

7. Select the following features and then click on **Next** as shown in the following screenshot (note that you can always add more features later when you require them):

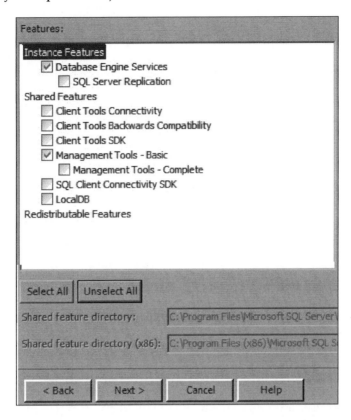

- ○ **Database Engine Services**: This will install the basic database engine only, which will allow us to create the database. However, this will not allow us to manage the database.
- ○ **Management Tools – Basic**: This will install the Studio Management tool that will allow us to interact with the DBMS, create databases, drop databases, add users, and so on.

8. Next, we need to set up the database instance. In the **Instance Configuration** dialog, select the **Named instance** option and then type sdedb; use the same name for the **Instance ID** field. You may not have any installed instances, and that's fine. This will also show you the existing instances if you already created ones before. As you can see in the following screenshot, I currently have an existing instance called **SQLEXPRESS** installed on this machine:

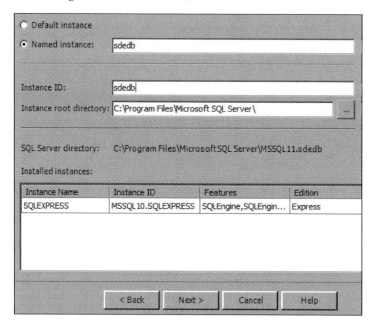

9. Click on **Next** to move to the next page. In this page, we can use specific Windows user accounts to manage the database. It is recommended that you use a dedicated Windows account to manage the database and all other database services. However, for simplicity, we will leave this to the default values as applied in the following screenshot and then click on **Next**:

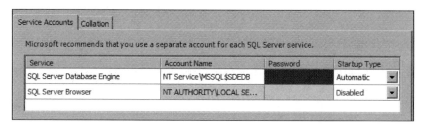

The following screenshot illustrates the database engine configuration. It is a very important step. This is where you set the authentication mode: whether you want to allow access control using Windows authentication or SQL Server authentication.

10. Select the **Mixed Mode** option as it gives us better control.

11. Enter a password for the default `sa` user, which is the master system administrator user that we will use to manage and add users. Make sure that you remember the password because we will use it later.

12. Leave the rest of the configurations to their default settings and then click on **Next**, as shown in the following screenshot:

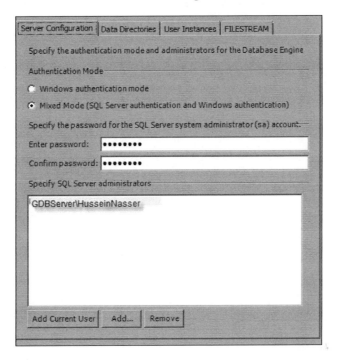

13. In the **Error Reporting** dialog, use the default values and click on **Next** to commence the installation. This will take a while; once it is complete, you will see the following status messages:

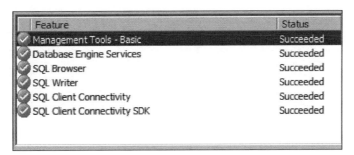

14. Click on **Close**; you have finished installing SQL Server Express.

Configuring SQL Server Express

You just installed SQL Server Express; you now have a database server running on this machine. Now, it is time to configure the database so that we can remotely connect to it and add users.

Enabling TCP remote pipe

TCP remote pipe is another term for the networking capability that is available in SQL Server. This feature allows remote connection from other machines to the database server in order to manage and control the database. By default, remote connections are disabled for Express, so we can't connect to the database unless we enable the remote connections. In the **Start** menu, point the cursor to **Microsoft SQL Server 2012**, **Configuration Tools**, and then click on **SQL Server Configuration Manager**, as seen in the following screenshot:

Now, we need to configure the TCP remote pipe to enable remote access. To do this, perform the following steps:

1. From the tree nodes, expand **SQL Server Network Configuration**.
2. Click on the **Protocols for SDEDB** option; this is the instance we created.
3. From the panel on the right-hand side, enable TCP/IP by right-clicking on the node and selecting **Enable**. You will be notified to restart your service— we will get to that in a bit. Click on **OK** to close the message.

4. Right-click on **TCP/IP** and select **Properties**.

5. In the **TCP/IP Properties** dialog, activate the **IP Addresses** tab.

6. Scroll down to the **IPAll** section.

7. Set the **TCP Dynamic Ports** field to blank and the **TCP port** field to `1433`.

8. Click on **OK** to save the changes.

Look at the following screenshot for details:

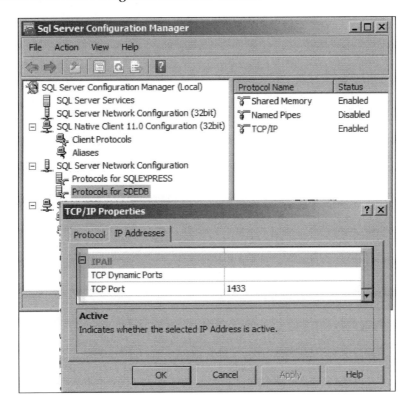

After making these changes, we have to restart the service so that it takes effect. In the Configuration Manager, click on **SQL Server Services**, right-click on **SQL Server (SDEDB)**, and then click on **Restart**, as illustrated in the following screenshot:

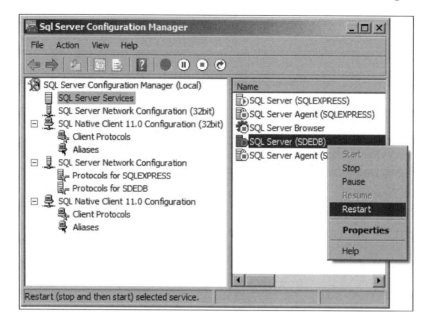

You have now enabled remote access to your database. Next, you will learn how to connect and manage your database.

> Make a note of how I keep saying database and not geodatabase. The reason is that this database is not yet enabled for geographical operations. We will learn how to enable it later in this chapter.

Enabling the firewall's database port

As you must have noticed in the previous section, the port 1433 is responsible for exchanging information between the client and database server. So, naturally, this port should be enabled on the server machine for packets to pass through it. I really hope you are not one of those users who disable the firewall completely just to allow a single application to pass through. Disabling the firewall is never a good idea unless you know what you are doing; always spend more time to configure your firewall rather than taking the easy way out by shutting down the entire protection.

Perform the following steps to enable the SQL Server port on the database server:

1. In GDBServer, click on **Start**, type the WF.msc command, and then hit the *Enter* key.

2. In **Windows Firewall with Advanced Security**, click on **Inbound Rules**.

3. From the **Action** menu, click on **New Rule**.

4. In **New Inbound Rule Wizard**, select **Port** and then click on **Next**, as shown in the following screenshot:

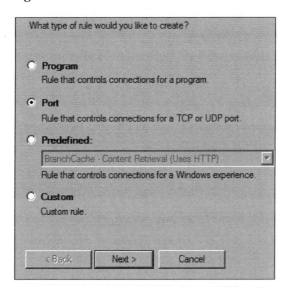

5. Select **TCP protocol** and set the **Specific local ports** option to 1433 as shown in the following screenshot; then, click on **Next**:

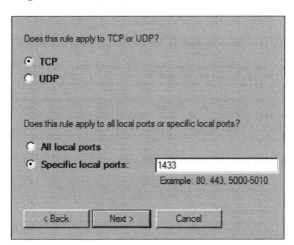

6. As seen in the following screenshot, select **Allow the connection** to allow all connections coming from port 1433 and then click on **Next**:

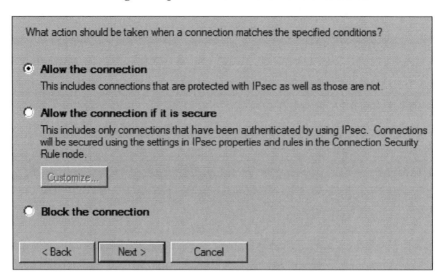

7. Apply the connection to all workspaces, **Domain**, **Private**, and **Public**, and then click on **Next**. You can put some restrictions to avoid public connections so that people from outside your network cannot connect to your database. This is clearly described in the following screenshot:

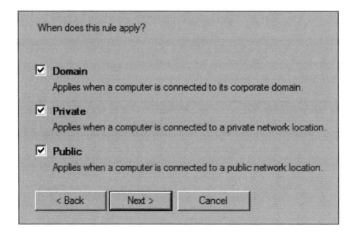

8. Finally, give a name and description to the port rule and click on **Finish**, as shown in the following screenshot:

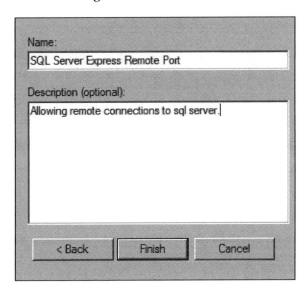

We have enabled the firewall port; now, we can safely connect to the database.

Connecting to the database

During the SQL Server Express setup, you have also installed the SQL Studio Management tool. This tool allows you to connect to the database using the administrator credentials you specified during the setup. In the Studio Management tool you can manage the database, create databases, manage logins, grant privileges, and so much more.

We will now connect to the database server, GDBServer, from within the same machine. So, it should work even without the firewall rule. From the **Start** menu, expand **Microsoft SQL Server 2012** then click on **SQL Server Management Studio**, as illustrated in the following screenshot:

You will be prompted with a **Connect to Server** dialog; in the **Server name** field, type your database server's name—mine is GDBServer. Then, select **SQL Server Authentication** from the **Authentication** drop-down list. In the **Login** field, type sa—this is our system administrator. I hope you remember the password you set in the setup because you are going to use it now. Type the password and then click on **Connect**. The following screenshot illustrates this:

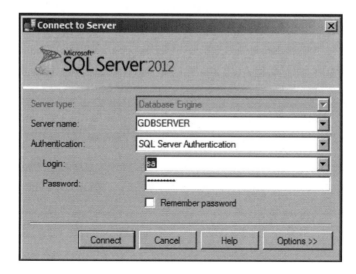

Once you are successfully connected, the **Object Explorer** tab in the left-hand side will be populated as you can see in the following screenshot. The **Databases** node contains a list of databases configured on this instance whereas the **Logins** node contains the users who have access to this instance. We will learn later how to add a user.

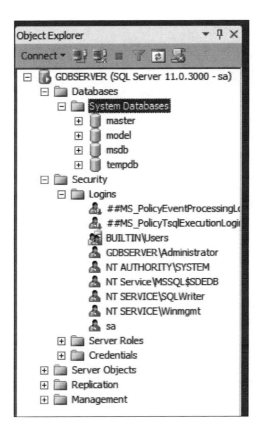

Connecting to the database from a remote machine

The steps for connecting to the database server are exactly the same as the steps explained in the previous section. However, in order to connect to the database, you will need the SQL Server Management Studio tool. You can use the same installer, SQLEXPRWT_x64_ENU.exe, on the machine you want to connect from and then specify the **Management Tools – Basic** feature as explained in the following screenshot:

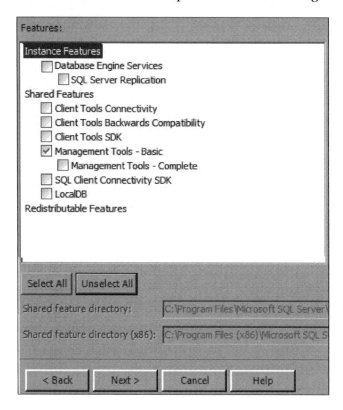

Creating an enterprise geodatabase

This is the step we have all been waiting for; now that our database is fully configured and ready, it is time to coat it with the geodatabase flavor. For this, we need a machine with ArcGIS for Desktop installed; you can use the same machine you worked on during the course of this book. You will need to install the basic management tools from the Microsoft SQL Server Express 2012 installer.

For details, refer to the *Connecting to the database from a remote machine* section.

You can also install ArcGIS for Desktop on your database server and carry on with the exercises.

After installing SQL Server Management Studio, make sure you can connect to the database at GDBServer. Once you are able to connect successfully, we can start creating the geodatabase. To do so, perform the following steps:

1. Open **ArcCatalog** and activate **ArcToolbox**.

2. Expand **Data Management Tools** and **Geodatabase Administration** and then double-click on **Create Enterprise Geodatabase**, as illustrated in the following screenshot:

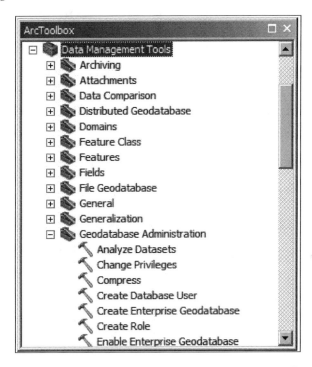

3. In the **Create Enterprise Geodatabase** dialog, select **SQL Server** from the **Database Platform** drop-down list because we are creating a SQL Server Express geodatabase.

4. The instance is the server name. Type in the machine name of your database server; mine is GDBServer.

5. Type in the name of the database; if you remember, our database was created during the setup, and it was SDEDB.

6. Leave the **Operating System Authentication (optional)** checkbox as unchecked because we will connect with named database users.

7. In the **Database Administrator (optional)** field, type sa and enter the password in the **Database Administrator Password (optional)** field.

8. Make sure that you check **Sde Owned Schema (optional)**; by doing this, we ensure that our geodatabase is owned by the SDE user that this process will automatically create.

9. Type the password of your SDE user and select the authorization file. The default password settings require the user to create a challenging password, and to avoid throwing an error, they must use a mix of alphanumeric characters. For instance, try Sd3P@$$w0rd. All this is illustrated in the following screenshot:

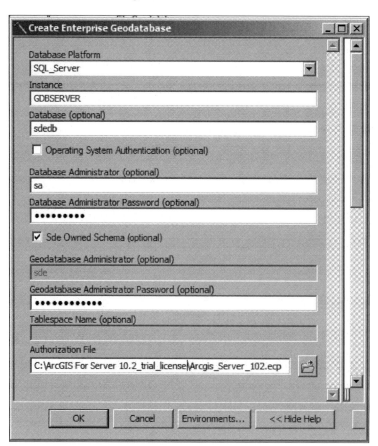

You should get a clean **Completed** dialog with no red messages, which looks like the dialog in the following screenshot. This indicates that your geodatabase has been created.

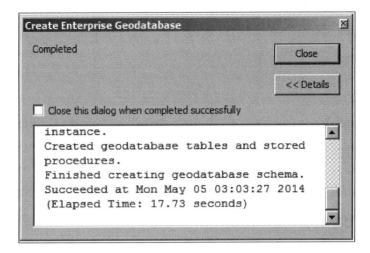

Working with an enterprise geodatabase

We can start working on our geodatabase after we have successfully created it. In this section, we will add some database users, create a geodatabase connection, and then migrate a file geodatabase to the new enterprise geodatabase.

Adding users

Now that we have successfully created the geodatabase, it is time to create some users. We will use these users to connect later. To create a user on the database, perform the following steps:

1. Connect to the database using SQL Management Studio.

2. Expand **Security**, right-click on the **Logins** node, and then click on **New Login**.

3. In the **New Login** form, type robb in the **Login name** field.

4. Select **SQL Server Authentication** and type the password for **robb**.

5. Uncheck the **Enforce password policy** checkbox so that we can use simpler passwords.

6. In the **Default database** drop-down list, select **sdedb**. Don't click on **OK** yet; we still have to map robb to sdedb so that the user is able to access the database. This is illustrated in the following screenshot:

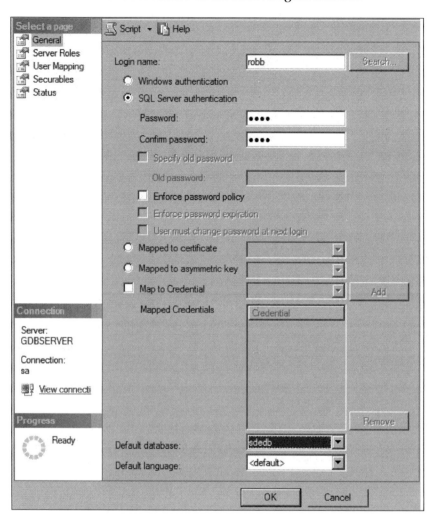

7. From the pane on the left-hand side of the dialog, click on **User Mapping**.

8. Check the **sdedb** record and type sde in the **Default schema** column as shown in the following screenshot:

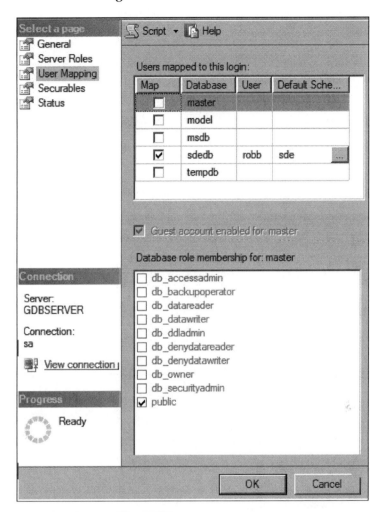

9. Click on **OK** to save the changes. Similarly, add the users Joffrey, Tyrion, and Dany.

Creating a connection to the enterprise geodatabase

A geodatabase connection is a channel that is established between ArcGIS and the enterprise geodatabase. To create a connection, we need to specify the database server and the user credentials. Without this information, we will not be able to create a connection. To create a geodatabase connection using the SDE user, perform the following steps:

1. Open **ArcCatalog** and expand the **Database Connections** dialog from the **Catalog Tree** window.

2. Double-click on **Add Database Connection**.

3. From the **Database Platform** drop-down list, select the database; ours is **SQL Server**.

4. In the **Instance** field, type the name of the server; here, it is GDBServer.

5. Select the **Database authentication** option from the **Authentication Type** drop-down list and type in the SDE credentials.

6. Click on the **Database** drop-down list. This should be populated automatically as you leave the password field. Select your geodatabase.

7. Click on **OK** and rename the connection to sde@gdbserver. This is illustrated in the following screenshot:

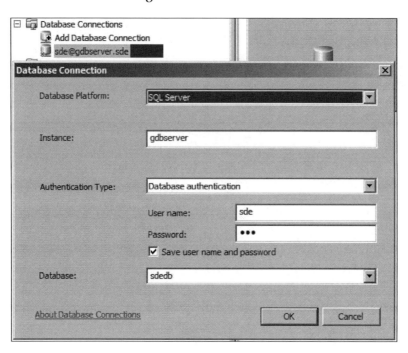

The type of geodatabase connection depends on the roles assigned to the user. Connecting with the `sde` user will grant you full access to the geodatabase, where you can copy, delete, and change almost anything.

 Use the skills you have acquired to create a feature class, add attributes, and work with a geodatabase as if it is a file geodatabase. Refer to *Chapter 1, Authoring Geodatabases,* for a walkthrough.

Create four more database connections with the users `Robb`, `Joffrey`, `Tyrion`, and `Dany`. Give them proper names so we can use them later.

Migrating a file geodatabase to an enterprise geodatabase

We have our enterprise geodatabase. You might have created a few feature classes and tables. But eventually, our clients at Belize need to start working on the new geodatabase. So, we need to migrate the `Bestaurants_new.gdb` file to this enterprise geodatabase. This can be done with a simple copy and paste operation. Note that these steps work in the exact same way on any other DBMS once it is set up. You can copy and paste from a file geodatabase to any enterprise geodatabase using the following steps:

1. Open **ArcCatalog** and browse to your `Bestaurants_new.gdb` geodatabase.

2. Right-click on the **Food_and_Drinks** feature class and select **Copy**, as seen in the following screenshot:

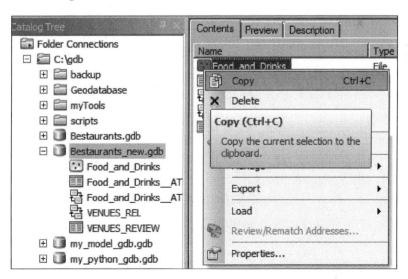

3. Now, browse and connect to **sde@gdbserver**; right-click on an empty area and click on **Paste**, as seen in the following screenshot:

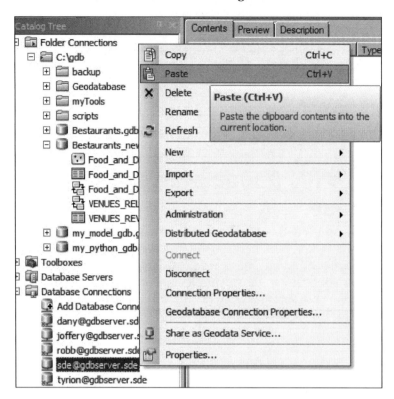

4. You will be prompted with a list of datasets that will be copied as shown in the following screenshot. Luckily, all the configurations will be copied. This includes domains, subtypes, feature classes, and related tables as follows:

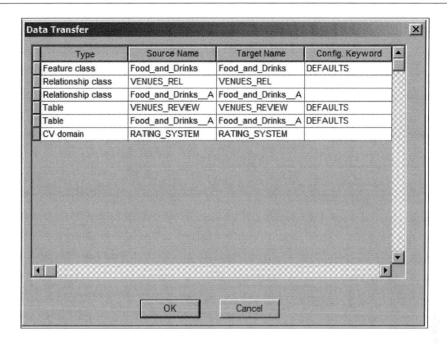

5. After the datasets and configurations have been copied, you will see all your data in the new geodatabase. Note that in an SQL Server enterprise geodatabase, there are two prefixes added to each dataset. First, the database is added, which is `sdedb`, followed by the schema, which is `SDE`, and finally the dataset name, as shown in the following screenshot:

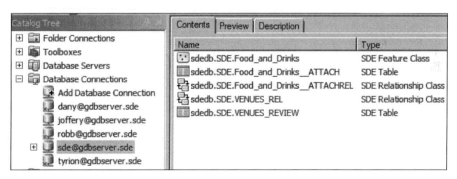

Assigning privileges

Have you tried to connect as `Robb` or `Tyrion` to your new geodatabase? If you haven't, try it now. You will see that none of the users you created have access to the `Food_and_Drinks` feature class or any other dataset. You might have guessed why. That is because `SDE` has created this data, and only this user can allow other users to see this data. So, how do we allow users to see other users' datasets? This is simple: just perform the following steps:

1. From **ArcCatalog**, connect as **sde@gdbserver**.

2. Right-click on the **sdedb.SDE.Food_and_Drinks** feature class, point the cursor to **Manage**, and then click on **Privileges** as shown in the following screenshot:

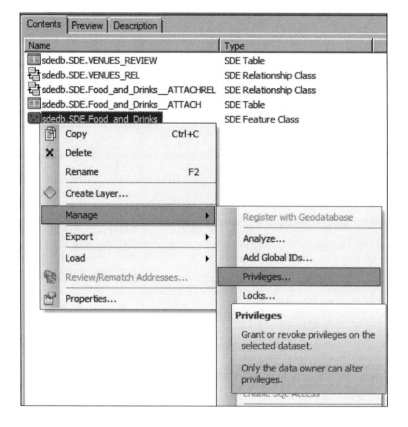

3. In the **Privileges...** dialog, click on **Add**.

4. Select all four users, **Robb**, **Joffrey**, **Tyrion**, and **Dany**, and click on **OK**.

   Make sure that the **Select** checkbox is checked for all four users, which means they can see and read this feature class.

5. For **Dany**, assign **Insert, Update**, and **Delete** so that she can also edit this feature class, as shown in the following screenshot.

6. Apply the same privileges to all other datasets as follows and click on **OK**.

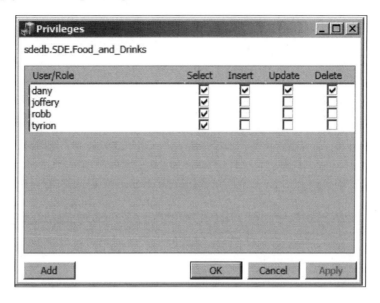

Try connecting with `Robb`; you will now be able to view all datasets. You can use Dany's account to edit your geodatabase using ArcMap. You can create more viewer users who have read-only access to your geodatabase but cannot edit or modify it in any way.

Summary

This was a lengthy and rich chapter full of practical exercises. Enterprise geodatabases are an excellent choice when you have a multiuser environment. In this chapter, you learned how to set up, configure, and fully build your own enterprise geodatabase. You have used SQL Server Express as a relational database management system's backend, enabled remote access, and configured a number of users. Then, you created your geodatabase on top of the database instance. You then learned how to create a geodatabase connection using ArcCatalog to the new enterprise geodatabase. You migrated your file geodatabase, which you have authored during your journey through *Learning ArcGIS Geodatabases*, into a fresh enterprise geodatabase. Finally, you assigned different privileges to each user and access control to your new enterprise geodatabase.

This is the end of the book; let's recap what we have done during the course of this journey. We started with learning the concept of geodatabases. You might have noticed that we focused on file geodatabases and not the personal MS Access. The reason I made this decision is because file geodatabases will have more support and you can work with them even after a number of years, whereas personal geodatabases are being discontinued in the next releases of ArcGIS because of their dependency on Microsoft Office 2003 32-bit and their size limitation, which cannot exceed 2 GB. It has already been discontinued from ArcGIS for Server, and I doubt that if you picked up this book after three years, you will have the option to use personal geodatabases.

In *Chapter 1, Authoring Geodatabases*, we worked with a case study project called Bestaurants, created a geodatabase from scratch, added feature classes and attributes, and set the spatial reference so that we project our data correctly. We edited the geodatabase and populated these feature classes using ArcMap. In *Chapter 2, Working with Geodatabase Datasets*, we introduced new dataset types such as subtypes, domains, and relationship classes and used them to make our geodatabase richer. Then, we completely remodeled our geodatabase in *Chapter 3, Modeling Geodatabases*, where we learned that our initial design was a bit rigid and complex, so we simplified it using the UML visualization tool. We created a completely new simplified Bestaurants geodatabase. Our geodatabase became sturdy and consistent, and the client has been using it and adding features to it. That's why we had to introduce some optimization tools in *Chapter 4, Optimizing Geodatabases*, that will help us maintain a good and healthy geodatabase. We have been using the graphical user interface in ArcMap and ArcCatalog to work with our geodatabase; it was time to dive into more advanced tools. This is when we introduced scripting in *Chapter 5, Programming Geodatabases*, where we used Python to programmatically work with geodatabases. Using Python, we built a complete script to back up our Bestaurant geodatabase on a daily basis. Finally, in *Chapter 6, Enterprise Geodatabases*, we took a leap by using an upgraded version of a geodatabase, which is called an enterprise geodatabase. While setting up and configuring an enterprise geodatabase is challenging, working with the enterprise geodatabases in ArcCatalog and ArcMap is similar to working with file geodatabases, with minor differences that were highlighted throughout the chapter.

Index

model, creating 103-107
model, running 109

N

new attributes
adding, to feature classes 26

O

object tables
about 34
creating 34-38

P

proposed geodatabase model
about 54, 55
attachments in feature class,
enabling 62, 63
authoring 56
datasets, creating 57-60
geodatabase attachment 55
subtypes, adding 61
subtypes, types 61, 62
Python 85
Python scripting
arcpy commands 100-102
feature class, creating 91, 92
features, copying 94
fields, adding 92, 93
fields, deleting 92, 93
geodatabase, creating 89, 90
URL 86-89
using 86
web Bestaurants geodatabase,
backing up 95-99

R

relations
review, adding 41, 42
working with 38-41
relationship class
about 36
creating 36, 38

S

schema 9
shape files
importing 46, 47
Simple peer-to-peer relation 38
spatial index
about 70, 74
adding 75
spatial reference
about 13
URL 13
SQL Server Express
configuring 118
system requirements 113
SQL Server Express configuration
database connection 123, 124, 125
database connection, from remote machine
126
firewall database port, enabling 120-123
TCP remote pipe 118-120
SQL Server Express geodatabase
installing 114-117
subtype, feature class
about 25
adding 32
symbology 21

T

TCP remote pipe
enabling 118-120

U

Uncompress tool 102
users
adding, to enterprise geodatabase 129-131
users' datasets
performing 136, 137

W

web Bestaurants geodatabase
backing up 95-99

Thank you for buying
Learning ArcGIS Geodatabases

About Packt Publishing

Packt, pronounced 'packed', published its first book "*Mastering phpMyAdmin for Effective MySQL Management*" in April 2004 and subsequently continued to specialize in publishing highly focused books on specific technologies and solutions.

Our books and publications share the experiences of your fellow IT professionals in adapting and customizing today's systems, applications, and frameworks. Our solution based books give you the knowledge and power to customize the software and technologies you're using to get the job done. Packt books are more specific and less general than the IT books you have seen in the past. Our unique business model allows us to bring you more focused information, giving you more of what you need to know, and less of what you don't.

Packt is a modern, yet unique publishing company, which focuses on producing quality, cutting-edge books for communities of developers, administrators, and newbies alike. For more information, please visit our website: www.packtpub.com.

Writing for Packt

We welcome all inquiries from people who are interested in authoring. Book proposals should be sent to author@packtpub.com. If your book idea is still at an early stage and you would like to discuss it first before writing a formal book proposal, contact us; one of our commissioning editors will get in touch with you.

We're not just looking for published authors; if you have strong technical skills but no writing experience, our experienced editors can help you develop a writing career, or simply get some additional reward for your expertise.

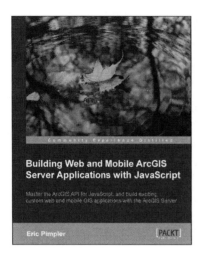

PUBLISHING

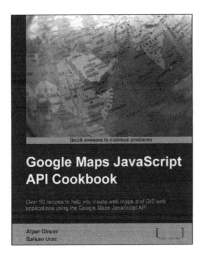

Google Maps JavaScript API Cookbook

ISBN: 978-1-84969-882-5   Paperback: 316 pages

Over 50 recipes to help you create web maps and GIS web applications using the Google Maps JavaScript API

1. Add to your website's functionality by utilizing Google Maps' power.

2. Full of code examples and screenshots for practical and efficient learning.

3. Empowers you to build your own mapping application from the ground up.

Administering ArcGIS for Server

ISBN: 978-1-78217-736-4   Paperback: 246 pages

Installing and configuring ArcGIS for Server to publish, optimize, and secure GIS services

1. Configure ArcGIS for Server to achieve maximum performance and response time.

2. Understand the product mechanics to build up good troubleshooting skills.

3. Filled with practical exercises, examples, and code snippets to help facilitate your learning.

Please check **www.PacktPub.com** for information on our titles

Made in the USA
San Bernardino, CA
06 February 2017